NATIONAL IDENTITY

NATIONAL IDENTITY

CONFESSIONS OF AN OUTSIDER

SIMON BRIDGES

HarperCollins*Publishers*

The publisher acknowledges Faber and Faber Ltd for their permission to quote from 'This Be the Verse', in the volume *High Windows* by Philip Larkin.

HarperCollins*Publishers*
Australia • Brazil • Canada • France • Germany • Holland • Hungary
India • Italy • Japan • Mexico • New Zealand • Poland • Spain • Sweden
Switzerland • United Kingdom • United States of America

First published in 2021
by HarperCollins*Publishers* (New Zealand) Limited
Unit D1, 63 Apollo Drive, Rosedale, Auckland 0632, New Zealand
harpercollins.co.nz

Copyright © Simon Bridges 2021

Simon Bridges asserts the moral right to be identified as the author of this work. This work is copyright. All rights reserved. No part of this publication may be reproduced, copied, scanned, stored in a retrieval system, recorded, or transmitted, in any form or by any means, without the prior written permission of the publisher.

A catalogue record for this book is available from the National Library of New Zealand

ISBN 978 1 7755 4196 7 (pbk)
ISBN 978 1 7754 9227 6 (ebook)

Cover design by Mietta Yans, HarperCollins Design Studio
Cover photography by Garth Badger
All other photographs are supplied courtesy of the Bridges family collection
Printed and bound in Australia by McPherson's Printing Group
The papers used by HarperCollins in the manufacture of this book are a natural, recyclable product made from wood grown in sustainable plantation forests. The fibre source and manufacturing processes meet recognised international environmental standards, and carry certification.

For Natalie

Six-year old me, circa 1982, dressed up as a pretty lady by my older sisters, make-up and all.

Contents

Introduction   1

1. Race   7
2. Nationality   22
3. Class   38
4. Masculinity   54
5. Marriage   72
6. Fatherhood   89
7. Introversion   104
8. Politics   119
9. Education   136
10. Crime   154
11. Food   175
12. Music   192
13. Nature   209
14. Social Media   225
15. Worldview   242
16. Religion   257

Conclusion   273
Notes   277

INTRODUCTION

I LOVE NEW ZEALAND. I LOVE IT MORE THAN ANYWHERE ELSE because it's mine, the place of my forebears and my descendants. But no country is perfect. There are aspects of our national character that frustrate me, annoy me and downright make me angry. If we think of New Zealand as better than everywhere else, that indicates a complacency and smugness. And that holds us back.

The title of this book is of course something of a dad joke. But it also marks a serious attempt to question myself and the country I live in. I'm not suggesting some bout of self-doubt or self-loathing. Far from it. I simply want to strip back our collective self-satisfaction and take a good look at a few facets of our identity, often through my own story. New Zealand can be even better. And if we can be, we should be.

One dictionary definition in my big old *Collins* says identity is *the state of having unique identifying characteristics held by no other person or thing*. I like that. You and I have unique identities, and I explore mine here in this book. I also explore our national identity.

To use a terrible but useful phrase, I've gone on a personal journey. I'm still very much on it. Who I am today is different to who I was as a youngster or a young lawyer. I suspect this will also be true in another decade and then in the decade after that. My identity has and will continue evolving. As my old mate Lockwood Smith once said, those whose views haven't changed over the years shouldn't be proud, they should be dejected. If we aren't moving with the times and evolving to changed circumstances to at least some degree, we are numpties.

I have come to realise I see myself as different, an outsider. Being Māori puts me in the minority, and yet for much of my life I also haven't felt properly Māori or accepted as such. The same is true with my British heritage – so strong in my DNA, but on the other side of the world I am not comfortably accepted in any camp. Not fitting in, whether at law school or rugby games, has left me simultaneously wanting to lean in and withdraw. I bet I am not alone here.

In this book I have sought to be faithful to what is true and what I actually feel and believe. Sometimes this is against my own interest, as I let you know of my cowardice and lack of physical prowess or admit what a tool I made of myself trying to get into law firms and how hurt I was when the media mocked my lack of elocution. But there is no point in trying to be someone else just because it might be bad for 'my brand'. Life is too short – and who cares anyway. To quote a great lyrical expression of that ethos, Anthony Kiedis sings, 'I am what I am; most mother%$kers don't give a damn.'

Every chapter in *National Identity* addresses something that has had a profound effect on who I am and what I believe. I begin with race and my Māori whakapapa. My experience is a feeling of otherness for being Māori, and yet an otherness from other Māori. Too Māori and not Māori enough. It's taken me time as an adult to work all this out and feel comfortable with who I am in my own skin. I am not alone in this – far from it. New Zealand itself is still working this out.

I also deal with my nationality, and specifically another massive chunk of my whakapapa: my Englishness. It's cringeworthy today to speak of 'home' back in the United Kingdom, but my roots to that place a million miles away go back millennia. I take my English ancestry with me like an imaginary friend wherever I go, but I also wonder how much the fact of it really matters anymore.

In our national consciousness we still hold on to a view that we are an egalitarian nation – better and fairer than most other places. Are we really? I reckon we are much more classist than we oh-so-self-contentedly think. While we don't have the explicit class divisions of Great Britain, we do have softer distinctions that grow like house prices by the day. In *National Identity*, I grapple with being raised working class and breaking into the upper reaches of our society, learning a few hard lessons along the way.

Chapter four is devoted to masculinity. According to our Kiwi culture, I've never quite been a 'real man', and I am sure there are many men who know this feeling too. A lightbulb went on for me when I realised that I am an introvert. Carl Jung thought that where you fit on the extrovert–introvert scale is the most important factor in your personality. I think he's right, and working out I was an introvert has massively helped my wellbeing. I no longer struggle to meet some extrovert ideal. Our idealised masculinity in New Zealand is of strong, physical, laconic men and I think we need to move on.

I also examine my relationship with my father. Dad is now in his late eighties and has dementia. But he was always an emotionally distant father, an island out at sea. If we are all a reaction to our parents, I certainly prove the point. I try, though, to parent differently to him and give more of myself emotionally and timewise to my children.

I have dedicated *National Identity* to my wife Natalie. Most of us have or have had partners, and just as people look more like their pets over time, so too do life partners. In my case, Natalie and I have become more similar, more integral to each other's lives, and have changed each other forever. A committed relationship refines and satisfies us. It makes us better people.

Politics, education, crime, kai, music, nature: these are the stuff of a life. Culturally, a lot has changed in recent times for New Zealand. In politics we've become less robust, more snowflakish. Moreover, people don't participate as much anymore, eroding our institutions and national life. On education, I believe we are in crisis. We are turning into Aotearoa, Lifestyle Nation, rather than one that places value on excellence. We're deluding ourselves if we think that we are world-leading in education; world-losing would be more accurate. With crime, while its causes can be complex, let's not think a bout of 'Kumbaya' is the answer. What do I reckon? That what worked in the past – deterrence – is still the primary answer. As for food, music and nature, even they've been caught up in identity politics of late. As I show, the world is a minefield, yet so enriching if we can manage the navigation. Anyone for a steak pie? I'm hungry.

Leaving real life, what about my life online? The all-pervading effect of social media is changing how we perceive ourselves and our tribes within society. While an Instagram post can be heartwarming, a Twitter pile-on can be devastating. I've seen this in my own career first-hand, as social media has destroyed me and then built me up again. I've also learned valuable lessons for life online, like that less is more and that our real worth and friendships come from the physical world.

Speaking of which, how is New Zealand placed in the big bad world? I liken the answer to an increasingly dangerous Tinder date. As I argue on just about every other page, we need to shake off our complacency about what's happening. History will judge us.

Finally, I touch on an intensely personal subject for me: religion. Growing up in a religious household, it's always been a *thing*. I tell you my family and personal story, and more broadly reflect on the decline of Christianity in New Zealand's Pākehā community to the point where Christians are the new pariahs in mainstream society. Meanwhile, many are going in for a pick 'n' mix spirituality fix. More complacency and smugness? I couldn't possibly comment.

To me, issues of identity pose some of the biggest questions of our time. Who am I? Who are we as a nation? Complacency and confusion are the enemies but, if we can work this out, there is a liberation that comes with it. This book lets me do that for myself and maybe helps you to do it for yourself, for ourselves, too.

1
RACE

IT WAS SUMMER AT MOUNT MAUNGANUI IN THE MID-2000S AND, after going to the beach most days, I was properly brown. I didn't bother with sunscreen then as much as I do today, hence the distinctive sunspots on my face, which cartoonists always exaggerate and which my mother sometimes offers to pay to have removed.

Anyway, on this particular summer's day I was crook as a dog. Feverish. I rarely went to the doctor but this time I needed to. I'd been off work for a couple of days, which was rare for me. Into the doctor's surgery I went – not my usual one – and down I sat to wait. I hadn't shaved since being unwell and was in a black hoodie that I still wear, though it's a little tighter round the middle these days (waste not, want not). Finally the Pākehā male doctor entered the waiting room. He was South African, and he looked me up and down. After that, he was pretty rude. He wasn't interested in my symptoms and made a comment that I was wasting his time.

I was affronted. At the risk of sounding like the politician I wasn't yet, didn't he know who I was? At that time I was a hotshot lawyer, one of the best. The youngest senior Crown counsel in our country, as approved by the Solicitor-General. I was categorised to do any criminal case for the Crown in the land. Police and lawyers deferred to me, and when I was in court, people listened. I had degrees up the wazoo, including a Master's from Oxford University (a BCL for the snobs among you, billed as the best common law degree in the world).

And then it dawned on me. He was treating me like a bloody Māori. I have no categorical proof of this, and you may think I am being overly sensitive, but I am sure of it. The medical practice covered a low decile, high Māori population. I wasn't suited and booted and clean-shaven. I didn't have my business card with my titles and string of degrees. The doctor had stereotyped me. Young, unshaven, hoodie, brown: Māori.

Growing up, I never thought of myself as Māori, which isn't surprising really. On the top shelf of the cupboard there was a korowai made by Dame Rangimārie Hetet, a relative of Dad's. And there were a few adzes and carvings and the like as well. But that's where they stayed: in the cupboard.

I remember as a kid in the 80s watching the news as a family: six kids, two parents, all crowded around the box on Gloria Avenue, Te Atatū North. We'd cheer when Koro Wētere, the Labour Party Māori Affairs Minister, came on. He was Dad's second cousin so we were famous. And you could tell: the two looked the same and clearly went to the same backstreet hairdresser, who let them keep going with their atrocious comb-overs.

Koro was clearly Māori, and I suppose Dad was too. But we weren't really Māori. Not really. Mum was blonde, from a dairy farm, and went to Waikato Diocesan School for Girls don't you know. And Māoris didn't do well. That couldn't be us. Yeah I tanned well, but I wasn't a Māori. Not really.

It's not surprising Dad never talked about it. His mum, Naku Joseph, met her white, rough-diamond husband, Alf Bridges, working at the Te Kuiti Tavern. Rumour has it he knocked her up and she begged him to marry her before they had their first child, Lorna. The stories I piece together about my grandmother portray her as a humble, kind, hardworking woman, whereas Alf had some charm but enjoyed the beer and racing rather too much. A hard man.

Recently I asked my dad about his parents. He has bad dementia today, but he did say that his father was bad to his mum, bullied her and never gave her enough money to feed the household. I've been told that their house in Frankton, Hamilton, was less than salubrious even for those days nearly a hundred years ago now. No wallpaper, very sparse. And if dinner wasn't on the table, there was hell to pay.

Naku also had to beg Alf not to name my dad Rangi when he came along in 1933. Whether this is apocryphal or not, I can't certainly say. She knew Heath needed an English name if he was to do well. She made it clear to her children, Lorna and Heath, that the Māori world wasn't for them. It was the Pākehā world in which winners dwell. Assimilate or, even better, be Pākehā.

So Dad went with that. Even before Dad got dementia, he wouldn't or couldn't remember much with detail. He'd blocked it out. There was nothing to remember about childhood or whakapapa as far as he was concerned. You get educated, make money and be a success, son. The unspoken assumption was: as a white person.

At school my view was that I was a white kid with brown skin. Not a Māori, not really. I mean, as a really young boy colour didn't matter at all. My best friend at Rutherford Primary was a Samoan Mormon boy, Orlo. Then there was Jimmy, Asian of some sort, I didn't know what, and his dad had the Te Atatū Four Square. Frank was a fair dinkum Māori, and the intriguing thing about him wasn't his ethnicity but that he was the uncle to another kid a year below us. I couldn't work that one out.

At some point ethnicity began to have some relevance. Today it's not okay in the more socially liberal inner suburbs of Auckland and Wellington to talk about being part-Māori, but that's what I was. Mum said I was maybe about an eighth. She didn't want it too high and was saddened by the fact none of her kids had blue eyes like she did. As my dad said, a little mud in a glass of water made it all brown.

He loved his little homilies. He would trot them out regularly and they've stuck in my head. Another favourite of his was on marriage: once you've caught the bus you stop running. That always made us laugh. And mum would elbow him in the ribs.

So when I felt sensitive about ethnicity and was asked point-blank about my heritage, then that's what I was, just one-eighth Māori. I remember telling people that an eighth wasn't very much. Probably just my feet. Then one of the kids, a white kid from what my mum would call 'a bad background', started calling me nigger toes. I didn't like that. And he was supposed to be my friend. My mum was blonde. I just tanned up a lot sometimes. I was white with brown skin, definitely.

A couple of years back, we six kids got my parents those DNA tests for their birthdays both in October – as both a bit of a laugh and to determine our ancestry once and for all. Heath and Ruth both spat into tubes and sent them off to Ireland for analysis. My mum's was simple: British through and through with a dash of Nordic, maybe from those marauding Vikings a long way back. Dad is a fair bit more exotic: twenty-nine per cent Polynesian (there is no specific Māori category), thirty-seven per cent European (Ireland, Scotland, England, Wales, Turkey and France all get a mention), and thirty-four per cent European Jewish. A third of each, for ease of explanation. I believe these tests to be pretty accurate. After all, the pathologist over in Ireland wasn't to know Dad is Ngāti Maniapoto, and the rest checks out. We knew of the Jewish roots, which are certainly on Dad's mum's side but also possibly on his dad's too. Some digging fills the picture out. My father's great-grandfather was Samuel Aaron Joseph, a London Jew whose Google search turns up surprisingly fruitful for someone dead so long. The *Australian Dictionary of Biography* places him as significant in both our country and across the ditch. Indeed, he's the first politician in my family tree that I am aware of (my grandfather Alf was a Hamilton city councillor in the 1930s). The Aussie dictionary states:

> Samuel Aaron Joseph (1824–1898), merchant, was born on 14 October 1824 in London, son of Aaron Joseph of Streatham and his second wife Frances, née Cohen. In January 1843 he arrived in the Prince of Wales at Wellington, New Zealand, and began in business. He became skilled in the Māori language and interpreted for Governor (Sir) George Grey when he pacified the Māoris.

It goes on to describe Samuel Joseph's merchant banking in Sydney, where he ran away to after little over a decade in New Zealand. There he became very prominent in banking, the synagogue and in politics. But what is left out of the biography is just as interesting, more so for our purposes. In addition to being fluent in te reo, a financial guru and an Aussie MP, it seems my illustrious forebear was also an inveterate rooter.

While in New Zealand, he had some help with his reo as well as with the internationally understood language of love from a couple of – *cough cough* – Māori common law wives. The story that seems to check out is that these relations started the Joseph and Hohepa lines, from which my grandmother Naku is descended, Samuel being her grandfather. This means Jamie Joseph, the famous Japanese rugby coach, while more coordinated and larger than my good self, is a relative; as is, from a different wāhine in Aaron Joseph's life, fishing legend Bill Hohepa. The two lines, Joseph and Hohepa, from the two wives.

In 2008 I became a Member of Parliament. In my maiden speech I dutifully outlined my Ngāti Maniapoto whakapapa. Yet the reality was that, as a thirty-two-year-old Kiwi male, I hadn't resolved in my head and heart what it meant to be brown on the outside, white on the inside, 'one-eighth Māori' or just plain Māori. In my defence I had been busy: constantly on the run from school to university, to overseas study, to law and to parliament. I hadn't had time to get deep and meaningful. But while the process wasn't immediate, politics can force these things out into the open if you stay long enough and go high enough. You have to confront who you are – you have to do the deep and meaningful. Something I had yet to do at that point in time.

Over time I began to feel I was too Māori to be Pākehā and too Pākehā to be Māori. Not a proper one, at least. Politicians and journalists could be rude about this. The day I became leader of National, senior journo Barry Soper commented that my claim to Māori heritage was incredibly shaky. He wrote that 'considering their new leader is just three sixteenths Māori' – where he got this from, I have no idea – any chance of getting the Māori vote was 'unlikely to wash.' He kept on in this vein over time, mocking my heritage, saying that I was not Māori enough.

In fairness, Barry was sniffing out my own discomfort and uncertainty. He was far from alone. What was I? There were entire columns dedicated to the issue, many negative. It was almost as if some would have preferred me to say I *wasn't* Māori, which would have not only been terrible politics but a grave sin against my forebears, my iwi and hapū. I was confused.

Certain politicians agreed with the commentators, effectively calling me an Uncle Tom. This was especially pronounced from New Zealand First bizarrely enough, given their schizophrenia on all things Māori and iwi. But it was also there subtly from the Labour MPs. If you can't speak te reo, you ain't a real Māori. And real Māori are Labour.

On marae, the receptions I've received have varied greatly. In my first term, as one of the few Māori newbies, I was placed on the Māori Affairs Parliamentary Committee and really enjoyed it. We toured marae all over the country, from South Auckland to the remote East Coast, eating good kai. I felt at home. But as I progressed career-wise and, particularly as I became leader of National, things understandably became more political. Rātana has always been cordial, friendly even. Whānau of mine, Morehu, led the building of the famous holy temple there. That warmth wasn't my experience at Waitangi though. Māori at both these events speak about how it's a time for bold truth-telling and anything can be said. But in my experience many don't seem to believe it, especially at Waitangi. Up north they certainly didn't want to hear my truths, maybe a little too home-truthsy, not in line with the same old tropes many tell year after year about honouring the Treaty, doing the mahi and giving Māori our fair share (much more than whatever was received the year before).

In my own neck of the woods, people have been much more accepting and kind. In Tainui and Maniapoto country, there's a sense that whānau is whānau, whatever his colours. One time when I was back at my home marae at Oparure, I took my wife and kids. What was remarkable for me was how my two boys, Emlyn and Harry, in particular, were affected by it. They just knew that they were home. Today still, they often talk about how their cousins made them welcome at 'our marae', and how one uncle showed them how to open mussels. Let's remember that my kids go to events with me on probably a fortnightly basis – it's another form of babysitting. But it's rare for them to ever talk about it again. Like I said, spiritually, they just knew.

Overall, my experience tells me that while I am less and less confused about my heritage, we as a nation are still deeply schizophrenic about our tangata whenua and about race more generally. The story I tell shows that this is certainly the case in my own family over the last century. From my grandmother, who grew up around a rural marae speaking fluent te reo, there has been an ambivalence – probably even hostility – to our ethnicity that is only now being thought through with complete honesty. In fairness to Naku Joseph, my father and even myself, hasn't this defensive posture been to protect ourselves? I don't think I am overly sensitive, but the reactions of the doctor in the Mount, my Pākehā mates at school, and others, tell a relatively clear story.

That though leads to many other problems. Naku, Heath and I are Māori. One can't deny reality. But what do I say when neither mainstream media nor Māori accept me entirely? I get that I don't speak te reo and that I am a Tory. I believe in many things that don't fit well with a traditional

Māori worldview — like individualism, capitalism and probably a few other -isms. My bloodline and whakapapa say one thing and, to many, my worldview says something else. I believe there are many Māori like me and therefore my story is an important one. In our hundreds of thousands we are in between, in no-man's land, yet Māori. We have no experience on a marae, no fluency with the language or cultural proficiency. Yet we are Māori.

Sociologists and historians — and Willie Jackson and John Tamihere — talk about the urbanisation of Māori and with it the dislocation experienced en masse from our culture, the process whereby the Nakus of this world moved from the rural marae to the city centres and lost connection. This meant that for the Heaths and Simons there was no hope of connection at all to our roots. It may be sad but I've never been sentimental; at a level, it is what it is. Government can and does chuck a lot of money at programmes to deal with this dislocation, whether for te reo teachers or cultural programmes in education and health, and frankly in our prisons as well. But in my view there is a lack of realism in thinking that every last West Auckland Māori will get back onto the marae. It isn't going to happen.

The numbers tell where the faultline is. About a quarter of a million Māori are on the Māori roll for voting purposes. They vote Labour and the Māori Party. Then there are roughly the same number of self-identifying Māori on the general roll. They are like me, voting for National at the same or higher rates than the general population. Māori who give me a hard time at Waitangi, or more generally because of my views, forget about these National-voting Māori. It seems to me they think such Māori are misguided and must be re-programmed to be a Māori roll kind of Māori. I say this is a nonsense. A Scotsman can be vegan, Bible-bashing, transgender, Satanist – and vote SNP, Labour or Conservative – and still be a Scotsman. A Māori likewise may conform to certain views of how Māori should be, but we are no less Māori if we don't like kina, are a libertarian or a corporate in New York. Or, heaven forbid, a National MP.

That old crocodile Winston Peters said it well in his parliamentary maiden speech back when dinosaurs still roamed the earth, 'I am a New Zealander, I am a Māori, and I am also a lawyer. New Zealand is not a monotonous garden where every flower is the same; it is a garden where the diversity of the blooms enriches the view.' I liked this so much I quoted it in my own maiden speech. New Zealand needs to become more comfortable with Māori generally. But we also need a more sophisticated view than Barry Soper's stereotypical one. Just as all Scots don't wear kilts, we can't just put Māori over there as the ones with te reo, moko and marae.

When I became the Member for Tauranga in 2008, I was the equal tenth (with Paula Bennett) Māori to win a general seat in New Zealand. The few before me are a bit of a who's who, including James Carroll, Winston, Sandra Lee and Georgina Beyer. To me, it's staggering that I was the tenth, given this was 2008, not 1908. Some of the reason for this was a misguided paternalism – some may say racism – where Māori more than 'half-caste' weren't allowed to stand in general seats from 1896–1967. But it is also a product of a country where Pākehā New Zealand, and even much of Māoridom, typecast Māori as tiki-wearing, leaving those like me in no-man's land with not even a 'plastic tiki'. Not Māori and not non-Māori in the eyes of others.

I've never seen myself as a 'Māori MP' but rather an MP who is Māori. Issues that could come before the Waitangi Tribunal are too limiting for me, and I am as interested in our general economic policies as much as I am in our view on a Waitangi report. Indeed, as a general seat MP I have to be 'more than Māori'. What an ethnically Chinese voter thinks is every bit as relevant as a Māori constituent, because they're both voters and New Zealanders.

What do I think about the Māori seats and the Māori wards that are becoming more and more fashionable for local government by the day? Well, I acknowledge the complexities because I know if you walk a mile (or a kilometre and a half) in another's shoes, there is a different view to mine that has some validity.

Let's be blunt: if I had a full face moko, Tauranga would not elect me as its MP. For the minority, the majority's rule can look a heck of a lot like tyranny. On the other side of it, the majority is democracy in its most basic form. As it stands, I won my general seat as a Māori man, and personally I wouldn't want to be in parliament or on a council as a diversity candidate because of my special status. I appreciate that MMP allows more diversity through its list system and of course the Māori seats also do for the foreseeable future. Preferential entry into things such as university or a corporate board is a can of worms, and I am not sure I have the heart to discuss that here. I did, however, apply to law school back in the mid-90s on the back of my whakapapa as well as a general application, 'just in case'. Fortunately I never needed to test this out, as my marks were good enough. But had I needed to, I am sure I would have got over my pride and come in by way of preferential treatment.

In parliament I sit next to Rawiri Waititi, Māori Party MP for Waiariki. He is a wonderful guy: warm, generous, strong and smart. We went to the same high school, Rutherford College in West Auckland, and in some regards we have much in common as Māori men. But I am willing to bet that our experiences at the same school could not have been more different. Rawiri would have been immersed in a world of te reo and tikanga under the tutelage of Dame June Mariu, a renowned Māori educator. I had zero to do with this, opting for different courses and instead enjoying school musicals, bands, speech contests and debating. In short, I steeped myself in Pākehā culture and I don't regret this. Today, Rawiri has a full face moko, which is beautiful and fierce and which I'm in awe of. But you couldn't pay me a billion dollars to get that done to myself. The pain would be one reason; the other is that it would change who I am – it's not me. Rawiri's tikanga is not a daily part of my life and never will be. Nevertheless, New Zealand needs to realise that I am just as Māori as Rawiri. Let's not look down on him, and let's not look down on me. He's not too Māori and I'm not too Pākehā. Let's celebrate the diverse garden.

As my life has continued, I have become increasingly comfortable with this. Funnily enough, it took my time at parliament to flush it out. Through experiences before politics and more often than not as an MP, I've faced personal trials and conflicts that have made me realise I am Māori for my own reasons, not because of what anyone else thinks.

I am learning te reo but only because I want to. If I prefer to read a book on French clocks rather than Te Kooti's last stand, I'm allowed. I have standing as Māori because of my forebears and bloodlines, and because as I have got older, I've realised it's who I am and I celebrate it. I am Simon Bridges and I am Māori.

2
NATIONALITY

NOW THAT YOU KNOW I AM MĀORI AND SELF-IDENTIFY AS SUCH, you also need to understand how important being British is to me – or more specifically, English. This is crucial heritage for me, the essence of who I am.

Let's clear up the possible pedants' points first. How can I be Māori and English? Well, that's not difficult is it? I am not like a car, like a Mazda or a Mercedes. I am more like a Labradoodle. I am Māori because it's my DNA and I identify as such; it's who I am. Likewise regarding my Englishness. We could get really complicated here, really pedantic. At one end of the spectrum, the argument is 'It's all identity' and at the other 'It's all bloodline'. For example, what do we think of the Grey Lynn tiki-wearing liberal who is one thirty-second Māori and spends all their time thinking about their Māori identity? I don't know, and that to me is at the margins.

Strictly speaking, if that person wants to vote on the Māori roll because they identify as Māori then they can legally. I have more important things to worry about. My good mate Paul Goldsmith clearly had it right though, recognising that just because one of his ancestors liked to knock about with Ngāti Porou wāhine, that doesn't make Paul 'Paora'.

For me it's straightforward. In blood terms, I am like one-sixth. That's significant. And so after that, I am not going to get too analytical. People perceive me as Māori and I understand myself in that way. Ditto my English ancestry. Three out of four of my grandparents are mainly English. I am English in ancestry, and that means a lot in terms of the blood flowing through my veins and my identity. While I may not be perceived as English, I certainly understand myself in that context. The history of the United Kingdom means a lot to me and how I see myself, my politics and my life.

The point about DNA and ancestry is worth dwelling on. I met my wife Natalie in Oxford seventeen years ago. We were both studying, for me law and for her, poetry of the Romantic period. We were at the same college, St Catherine's, in the Middle Common Room for postgraduate study. Romance was in the air and we quickly got together, as in a student environment of Greeks, Brazilians, Indians, Americans and every other nationality one can imagine, we shared the same Anglo-Saxon sense of humour. To show her how much I wanted her to come back to New Zealand, I asked Natalie, twenty-one at the time to my twenty-seven, to marry me. At the end of the year we married in a thousand-year-old chapel, with a student party after. Despite every wise person's view that we'd never last – I specifically recall the Canon of Oxford who married us trying to talk Natalie, in her youthful folly, out of marrying this swarthy Kiwi – three children later we've proved the critics wrong.

Natalie grew up in Coventry, in the Midlands of England – literally in the middle. As she says, the armpit of the country. To those of you who've ever thought at all about Coventry, you'll vaguely recall it had the crap bombed out of it in World War Two so the cathedral was partially destroyed. Outside of that, it has something to do with Lady Godiva – not the chocolates, but some naked bird on a horse who has a statue in the middle of town – and it has been a bit of an industrial hub for cars and military manufacturing in the past. Today, in all honesty, it's not a city I would put in Britain's top ten. But – and it's a very important but to me – her dad is a proud Welshman and her mother a Pole. Neither is a natural-born Coventrian. Taffy is so Welsh that he has leeks tattooed on his arm and loves rugby more than most Kiwis. Alicja, or Lidka, is so Polish that frankly I find her accent hard to understand. They've both grown on me. On this basis I like to tell Natalie: I. Am. More. English. Than. You. Are.

Again, we could get academic and pedantic here about the differences between ethnicity, nationality and identity; we could even get into discussion on citizenship and residency. I could probably entertain a long discourse on St Paul, whose Roman citizenship by birth rather than purchase entitled him to a hearing before the Emperor, giving him time in an Italian jail to write much of the New Testament. However, let me spare you all that and note that, at its most basic, Natalie can retort (not that she has), 'But my three children and I have British passports, whereas you don't, sunshine.' In any event, I feel more English based on my ancestry than Natalie does, and some days certainly, I love the idea of England as much as or more.

When talking about DNA in the last chapter, I said that my mum's was pretty bread and butter British and a little Scandinavian. Her father was Robinson Baxter. He came to New Zealand after World War One because a girlfriend two-timed him and broke his heart. He worked building the railway between Waihi and Tauranga and saved enough to buy a dairy farm at the road that now holds his name just outside of Waihi off State Highway Two. Robin was from Barnoldswick, which today is in Lancashire but which he (and my mum) viewed as Yorkshire. He was a Yorkshireman. The oldest gravestone in the Barnoldswick Ghyll church cemetery is from one of his forebears, Christopher Baxter, and his family records confirm that the Baxters lived in this area from at least the sixteenth century, for several hundred years.

I adore this fact and actually it makes me emotional when I think about it. Robin and his ancestors stayed put there, as was almost entirely the case in the past when people didn't globetrot as we do today and instead lived and loved, quarrelled and queried, ate and drank, did everything in the one village. For centuries. Mine and my children's fabric was woven there, metaphorically and literally, since the Baxters were weavers in that cotton-milling town. I believe we carry some of that wherever we go. It's our place, our tūrangawaewae, the same way that the King Country is from Naku Joseph.

And yet, and yet. Next to no one in Barnoldswick would know this today. They wouldn't recognise me or my accent, which people poke fun at even in my own country. And so while I want and will Barnoldswick to be my tūrangawaewae – a place I have standing – a lingering worry for me is whether it in fact is. My roots, for sure. But do I have a claim to it in any sense? Not legally, maybe morally? I don't in truth know for certain, despite its hold on my identity.

Just as my family has changed from when Robin left England for a better life, so too has Barnoldswick. Now it is much more diverse ethnically and demographically, more Polish and Pakistani perhaps than Church of England or Bible Chapel in which my grandfather was brought up. Do those families have more of a claim to Britishness than me? Certainly it is their home and, for those whose families migrated in the middle of the twentieth century, they now have nowhere else to properly call home. Whereas the Poles in England now have legal rights to a passport and, as I've noted, my wife and kids do, I don't. Those Polish folk as well as those from Armenia (think Dua Lipa), Greece (think George Michael before he passed away), and Trinidad and Tobago (to keep the music going, let's say Billy Ocean) all have and deserve passports in the UK, but I don't.

I do have somewhere else to call home – a few places actually. At Oparure marae near Waitomo, I still do have standing. Organising a visit is like herding cats, with protocols imposed and hoops to jump, but ultimately I know that when I am there I have a right to be there, and I return as a significant son for those who are proud of me and even for those who quietly see an Uncle Tom in their midst. Nevertheless, they can't deny me my standing. I also call Te Atatū home, where still today as a forty-four-year-old, I lived for over half my life and feel I know intimately. And finally there is Tauranga, where I have been for twenty years, have grown with, and have been a leader in. Perhaps it's greedy to lay claim to the UK as well?

Mum's mum, Dorothy Baxter née Goodwin, was a matronly woman who disapproved of Mum's prettiness and love of clothes and finery. Thinking about this still gets to my eighty-two-year-old mother, and while it amuses me at one level, it also shows me the distressing power of words in a child's life. Dorothy was born in New Zealand but her parents were from Derbyshire and Warwickshire, not too far from where my Natalie grew up.

And then there is Dad's side of the whānau. His father's family, before generations of working and boozing in Christchurch, were from Norwich. Even Naku's grandfather, as I've mentioned, was a London Jew. I'd love to know more about how far that goes back. Was his family living in the large Jewish community of Golders Green at about the time he left for New Zealand? I pictured a dandified Disraeli-like figure. Unlikely, but still.

My point on all of this is not that what I describe is uncommon – many of us are meat-and-three-veg Mr Bull Poms – but it is why I feel English and why this is important to me. My claim may not be strong today but still it's there within me. Mum used to talk about how her parents called England home. Now we find this quaint, or worse, cringey, just as some will be reading this homage to the UK from me as such. But where we come from really matters and this is where I come from and what was drummed into me. Even if Barnoldswick is no longer mine.

I don't subscribe to the view of life you sometimes see here in New Zealand that unless it's all tapa cloth and Dick Frizzell art, we can't celebrate it. To take such a view is as cringey as saying Britain is our be all and end all. Yes, we have an indigenous culture forged here and unique to us;

we should celebrate that. But those items of Kiwiana that consciously place us in the Pacific are oftentimes derivative and shaped by what came before and from elsewhere. For many of us that's our British, and in my case primarily English, heritage. My and many others' forebears brought that with them and we should be secure enough in our nationality today to say so.

Of course what has also happened is that we've become more clearly Pacific-oriented and Asian in our demography and disposition. It's exciting and may move our culture in ways many, including the media, don't foresee, for example with multiculturalism competing and possibly winning over against our Māori–Victorian Crown biculturalism. Suffice to say though, that right here and now, we all have our experience and background. Mine is a common one in our country, a meeting of Māori and British, and I take it with me wherever I go.

My mother used to frown on too much TV-watching: it was the Protestant puritan in her that I wear as a cloak around me to this day. As a mother of six in a time when mothers quite literally did it all, she didn't have much time for TV. With two exceptions: *Coronation Street* (before it became too saucy and everyone was bonking everyone else) and *Emmerdale*. The basic reason for this was that these shows portrayed home and reminded us where we came from. The

UK and, in *Emmerdale*'s case, Yorkshire. Mum also from time to time liked a bit of *Inspector Morse*, set in Oxford, and played by the inimitable John Thaw. I am sure now that this was a big part of why I went to Oxford. I knew my mother would be proud.

In fact, my heart had been set on US universities originally but, although I got into some top ones, the US exchange rate made the quest unachievable. While Oxford was the cost of a house in West Auckland or a substantial deposit for one, the US Ivy League colleges were Parnell or Ponsonby. But my mum's reaction was also a factor in my decision. I would have a Master's from Oxford; she knew what that represented in a way that she didn't for Cornell or Columbia.

My first trip to the UK was on my end-of-undergraduate-studies OE in 1999 with my then girlfriend. We went to London and Oxford, and they were everything I thought they'd be and more. New Zealand was so small and so, well, provincial. London was life! And the world. Whether Arab, Asian, Asiatic or Atlantic. Whether kebab, coffee, caviar or chamomile. I remember being shocked by full face hijabs all over Hyde Park while in awe of all the Bentleys and Lamborghinis at Marble Arch. Coming from Te Atatū North, I had never seen any of this before.

My next visit to the UK was as a Chevening Society Hansard Fellow. It was a generous junket that saw me 'work' at the Houses of Parliament and 'study' at the London School of Economics while living in a central London flat, drinking beer in the afternoons and evenings as an American girl and I worked our way through *The 100 Best London Pubs*. I loved every bit of it.

Then I went back for the year at Oxford. Again I loved it all, living at college and eating in halls with interesting people from around the world. I studied and partied heartily. But Oxford also taught me the cultural ambiguities of Britain. In many ways I see Britain as more similar to New Zealand than Australia, where there's an American-like confidence we don't possess. In Britain, class is always under the surface. Whether in the subtly cutting comment of a professor, where what isn't said to the silly antipodean is more important than what is. Or in my father-in-law's working class hatred of toffs because deep down he knows they would never ever let him into their elite circles, so why bother trying. Allied to this is a reserve I don't really like, certainly in the upper echelons. Whether in academia or with politicians I talked to, I would sometimes want to shake them and beg them to say what they *really* thought. Again, this was all unsaid.

In New Zealand, yes, we are changing. Housing and its cost is driving inequality and relative poverty like we have never seen before. But we are still, I believe, egalitarian – at the very least in an aspirational sense, if not entirely in reality anymore. I know that's far from good enough but at least we still have the belief. It doesn't matter who you're next to at the cricket or rugby – we can all talk to one another as equals. We also see the same health professionals and sit in the same waiting rooms as equals, my story in the previous chapter excepted. We all must rub alongside each other, mostly, as equals. And fundamentally we call spades spades. We are a fair, decent, straight bat sort of society.

At both the start of my time at Oxford but even more so by the end, I knew I must return to New Zealand. There were practical reasons why this had to be so. First and foremost, I owed bond money, which had paid for my Master's, to the law firm I had been working for in Tauranga. More than that, though, I was only at home in New Zealand – both in the positive and negative sense of this sentiment. Positively, I needed New Zealand and couldn't imagine living for long periods anywhere else. The land was in my heart and soul, as was the sand and the salt water and the rivers and the lakes. Whether it was the Waitākeres and West Coast beaches I grew up with or the Mount and its beach, New Zealand was me. And, as I have already mentioned, our people are a fair, decent people. As cheesy as it may sound, I also had a deep sense of patriotism and loyalty. I'd seen my father serve our local community as a clergyman and that to me was incredibly important. New Zealand had educated me and kept me healthy with a terrific public education and health system. The value of that came from our most decent of societies; people paid taxes for themselves and their families, and also for the wider community they were a part of. I knew before, during and after Oxford that I would go into the judiciary or politics. I was clear about this to Natalie – I was doing a Bachelor's of Civil Law (BCL) and had joined the National Party as a pimply teenager for very nationalistic reasons – public service here in my country, New Zealand.

Frankly, also, I had cultural cringe towards the UK. Deep down I wasn't sure I could foot it in a society so much bigger than the one I was from, where who you know is even more important if you want to rise to the top and contribute at the highest level. Every year a handful of Kiwis do the BCL at Oxford, and one in my year became a good friend. He stayed on, obtained what they call pupillage in one of the best commercial barrister chambers in London, and today makes, I am sure, millions of pounds with a lifestyle commensurate to that sort of income. He stays in touch with New Zealand through his exquisite Kiwi wine cellar, as good as any I've ever seen here, and by the occasional visit. He still supports the All Blacks but his life is in England. He is Pākehā. And never had the twang that I do.

It wasn't that I didn't think I could foot it intellectually. I believed I could, and Oxford showed me that. I kept up with the best of the best. But I couldn't see a brown man with freckles and Kiwi diphthongs, out of his cultural context, presiding over a London courtroom or as a Minister of State for the Conservative Party. Even in New Zealand I'd had to leave Auckland to pursue my deep desire of jury trial work. My uncle or granddad wasn't a judge or a former partner at Meredith Connell and my schools weren't right. I had no chance, without experience, of breaking into the big smoke in the early 2000s. Interestingly now, perhaps as if to prove me wrong in hindsight, a friend from school and Te Atatū church youth group is currently a first-term Conservative MP for Boris in the incredibly plummy seat of Guildford in Surrey. In any event, I felt positively drawn back to New Zealand as well as a sense of inferiority that I wouldn't make it in the UK.

As a New Zealand Minister of the Crown, when I visited the UK and when British pollies came here, I also got an undeniable sense of British condescension. Some MPs I met were brilliant and Boris Johnson fit into this category, being warmer and more engaging than I thought he'd be. More commonly though, the British political class found New Zealand minister visits both a tiresome chore and a chance for a little neo-colonial lecture. I recall meeting Zac Goldsmith, now Baron Goldsmith of Richmond Park, then Conservative MP (and less famous in these parts of the world than his sister Jemima, once married to cricket great and Pakistani PM, Imran Khan). He was reserved to the point of rudeness. I would have preferred he just didn't take the call than put us both through the awkward agony.

The same was true of his senior colleague at the time, Environment and Climate Minister Greg Barker, who used the meeting with myself and Lockwood Smith to talk down to us about how shit we were at climate change. This same lecture must be in the UK's general New Zealand talking points, because I've had it many times from Pommie politicians and diplomats and it smacks to me of a view that our country is a naughty little colony and to be told off like one.

As a rabid Anglophile I wouldn't mind this so much if we were still a friend with benefits. But in the period I was a minister I found a sad lack of British interest in our country despite our shared history, which contrasted with interest shown to us from other middle and large powers. The UK seemed far more EU-focused than Commonwealth-oriented. Ministers would feign interest for some of the meetings while their private secretaries fidgeted, as if impatiently waiting for the formalities with the colonials to be over so they could get back to business that mattered. That attitude did change, though, with an infamous referendum in the UK in 2016.

Brexit is like Donald Trump: a subject better not talked about in polite New Zealand company, so one-sided has the coverage and commentary here been. But one benefit for us parochially may be the return of some interest again, as we culturally share so much with the UK even if geographically we are so distant. Perhaps in the future we can hope for talking points with our Pommie counterparts that include more than a neo-colonial climate lecture.

As a way of holding on to my identity as British, I've championed a growing international Commonwealth movement called CANZUK through our parliament. I talk semi-regularly to mates in the UK, Australia and Canada. It's about growing cultural and economic bonds once again between countries we share so much with. Why couldn't we move freely between countries as if citizens, trade entirely freely (as we already do with our Australian cousins) and so on? Maybe it's a pipedream, but my sense of nostalgia as well as a sense of what could be possible again keeps me at it. Certainly as the world gets more dangerous, we should be calling on old friends in any way we can.

If I haven't made it abundantly clear yet, I bloody love the UK with its verdant green fields, pubs and toilet humour. I feel at home there while also sensing it isn't my home. There are many of us Kiwis of UK descent, and Kiwis married to Poms here and over there. Maybe if you fit this bill and identify with what I am saying about our conflicted identities, you'll be a bit like me and Natalie – unlikely to ever be perfectly happy in New Zealand or in the UK, always feeling that a little bit of you and what you need is in the other isle. But my home away from home isn't home. Barnoldswick isn't tangibly real in the same way that Te Atatū, the Mount and Oparure are. The UK is there in my dreams, as an imaginary friend I take with me, but when I wake up it is gone. My Vogels is buttered here.

I am a Māori, English Kiwi. The last word is probably most important – as whatever happens and wherever I go, that's my nationality till I die. However, they are all there, forming my identity.

3
CLASS

THERE IS NO DOUBT THAT NEW ZEALAND IS A FAR MORE egalitarian country than most. But that doesn't make New Zealand perfect. Some would say we don't have social and economic classes – and it's possible, but unlikely, that this was once true a long way back. Today, as the gap between the haves and have-nots has grown, it has loosely brought about class distinctions.

If your children live in a five-million dollar house in Remuera and go to a private school, they will mix with fewer children from less privileged backgrounds than ever before. This inevitably brings differences between demographic groups. There will still be *some* rubbing along together, but as people do less today by way of church and Rotary and sport, this gets smaller.

It's also true that, as we have become more and more

urban, these distinctions grow. The richest gal knows the poorest guy in Te Kuiti, not so much on the North Shore. The distinctions have probably always been around, but the scale of them at each end of the spectrum is greater than ever. With rampant house price inflation, this anti-egalitarian trend will continue to exacerbate.

That said, in contrast to somewhere like England, the class divisions are softer. We don't have lords and ladies on one side and chavs on the other, fixed in a set of structures that have existed for millennia. I remember at Oxford the clear chasm between 'townies' and 'gownies', the rough and the toffs. Believe me when I tell you the toffs were really toffy — so plummy, all the way to their pinkie signet rings — and the rough were *blaaady* rough. One evening Natalie and I went to the movies in Oxford town. We saw a bloke in white trackies who was beating a woman next to him. I looked around and decided I had to act. I stepped in, and to my surprise the guy stepped well back and his missus started yelling at me to 'mind my farken business'. She was about to start hitting me when Natalie pulled me away to our popcorn and colas. All class.

People left the UK to get away from all this, but nevertheless distinctions have still built up here in New Zealand on the basis of money, address and education. They exist like shades of a sunset melding into each other rather than distinct colours of a rainbow. It's not like that advert where the guy is appropriately wearing budgie smugglers on the beach but at a point it becomes not okay. There are working class and middle class and then those who are maybe more one than the other, but still a bit of both. It melds, and they are distinctions rather than stark divisions.

I was once reported in the media as saying that Natalie and I got on so well because we are both from working-class backgrounds. My family bristled at this, and there was a WhatsApp group chat among siblings who took offence and disputed this most unfair characterisation. Comical, in a way. Studies show most people's perception of themselves is middle-class. We all see ourselves in the middle, sometimes upper-middle, even when we ain't.

Natalie's upbringing was certainly British working class. Neither parent had been to university. Both did working-class jobs on working-class pay, and they lived smack-bang in a working-class street in the middle of working-class industrial Coventry, a safe-as-houses Labour seat. Natalie's dad, Taff, made cars and military hardware until the 80s, when in his view Thatcher shut it all down with her free market sink-or-swim economics. He despises all Tories to this day (please don't tell him about my day job; these days I describe myself to him as an author).

I accept at a level that my brothers and sisters are right in part — we weren't brought up quite as working class as Natalie. Dad, while from a relatively dysfunctional household that was certainly working class, went to university. He became a chartered accountant, was an auditor, and then obtained a Bachelor's of Theology after God spoke to him (see the chapter on religion). Mum, after her private-school education, went to Teacher's College and became a teacher as most 'ladies' did in her day – that or nursing. She really didn't teach though for most of her working years and was a terrific full-time mum to her six children.

So far then, not so working class. But these educational backgrounds disguise a few other things. As a Baptist preacher while we grew up, Dad, as the sole breadwinner, didn't earn much and we lived in working-class areas. Te Atatū Peninsula (then Tat North) has gentrified tremendously in recent years. Let's just say, when I was growing up there it hadn't. We lived in West Auckland and went to West Auckland schools and rubbed about with the kids of working-class people. It's also true that, while my siblings all lived in other areas before Te Atatū, as the youngest, I'm the only one who's entirely West Auckland born and bred. Maybe this accounts for my slightly different take than one or two of the older ones, who started life in the South Island and therefore don't sound as much of a Westie as me.

As another part of my case, my parents lacked any degree of worldliness or street smarts. They mixed with good, simple people. In all my life, my father has never touched a drop of alcohol. Fanta was his drink. My mum's idea back then of 'fancy', as she would say, would have been surimi cocktail. Neither would have known an hors d'oeuvres if you'd slapped one in their faces.

I am not knocking them, my siblings or anything about my upbringing. It was brilliant in its way. But while it was filled with ideas and values, it was also essentially unworldly, simple, working-class. We didn't know about business, politics, law, medicine, media or the arts. We didn't know anything about the ways of the big world and the people who made it happen.

To be clear, both my family and Natalie's had hoped for more from life. To think the opposite is a misconception about the working class. We do aspire. We believe and we dream. But we hadn't tasted the middle class, not yet anyway. This phenomenon is part of a profound change happening in Western politics today as the working class shifts right and our increasingly post-aspirational professional classes shift left. That, though, is a book in itself.

Because I was smart and worked hard, I got into Auckland Law School. Soon I began realising I wasn't like most of the rest of them there in the mid-90s. Different to today, nine out of ten kids from my high school didn't go to university. Smaller numbers progressed each year to sixth then seventh form (today, years twelve and thirteen) and then only a handful went to uni from the final year. Also unlike today, it was out of the question to go to a tertiary centre in a different city, particularly if you lived in Auckland. So from hundreds of kids in fifth form, we got to a hundred or so in seventh form and several who then went to university. I remember the careers counsellor actively discouraged me from going. In her view, polytechnic was where I should be. Law, she thought, was for me a bit ridiculous. So I was always going to be a bit different at law school. For starters, my mullet didn't fit in. The kids I grew to like and regard had gone to Kings and St Kents and Grammar and St Cuths. Their dads, mums, granddads or uncles were all lawyers or other professionals. And they didn't have mullets. So I worked to fit in. And after a time, the long hair went and I fit in a little more.

But it was more than the obvious bad haircut. The other students seemed to and know things in ways I didn't. They'd been brought up with a confidence and poise to know when to talk and when not to, and what to say when they did. I was all brain and no etiquette. This mattered at law school and even more as the race for summer internships and then full-time law clerkships heated up. And so I mimicked the kids from the best backgrounds and with the best skills and marks. They'd had a big headstart, but I could copy and learn.

I will never forget a little thing early on at law school, where somehow I was invited to a drinks function with academic staff and the then-Governor-General, a former Court of Appeal judge, Sir Michael Hardie Boys. I had at this time barely met many lawyers, let alone judges of our highest domestic court. Yet I bowled up to him bold as brass as he stood there in the academic common room with his military attaché. I can't remember what I said, but I was clearly too familiar. I talked to him like he was a mate on a Friday night down at Haddads, a local Westie burger and kebab joint. He turned his back on me like I'd shat on his shoe and I won't easily forget how I felt at that moment and for a time after. I was a loser from Te Atatū and I did not belong there. I didn't have any idea how to talk to someone like him in this context. It took me the entirety of my law school years to work all this out.

Until I got to a point of proving myself as a lawyer through raw grunt work and intellect, I sometimes felt a nagging sense of what many women in corporate life feel: imposter syndrome. I was a brown uncouth Westie. I didn't fit in. I was so far from cookie-cutter perfect, I wasn't even a biscuit.

Law school was hard, and I went through at the worst time. Bolger's government had imposed fees and interest on loans. My parents kept a roof over my head but could not contribute in any other way financially. I worked three part-time jobs late into the night before lectures the next morning at 8 am. Over time I worked out law and the legal method, winning prestigious competitions for courtroom technique and a senior prize in law for those in the top percentile for overall marks.

I appreciate there are many who've experienced much more otherness and, in fact, outright discrimination. I am no Āpirana Ngata, the first Māori to achieve a law degree, over a hundred years ago. Thousands of people paved the path for me. I was never flat out discriminated against. I am just saying that I was a working-class Māori Westie, and it wasn't all beer and roses making my way as an outsider. Some of that was economic and some was what I'd broadly call class.

I've already mentioned the mullet. In my first year, I saw an advert on a Student Job Search board in Auckland's quad, below Shadows bar (Remember those days?). It was for a wine steward at the Auckland Club. Back then there were two significant private clubs in Auckland and the Auckland Club was one of them, set back behind large wooden doors on Shortland Street. Think paintings, leather, staircases, nice finishings and libraries. I didn't have the foggiest about wine or cocktails or making cappuccinos from coffee machines, which were a relatively new thing then. But I applied for the role, and in the interview I made clear that if I had the privilege of getting the job, I would go from my bob-length haircut to a short back and sides. Well, that sealed the deal. I had finally got a haircut and a real job.

Five years later, I knew my shirazes from my grenaches and my G&Ts from my B&Bs – brandy and Benedictines, which some of the older members (particularly former Tauranga

Mayor Sir Bob Owens) enjoyed. The Club had been very good for me. Don't get me wrong, I certainly hadn't become a sophisticate, but the job had helped a boy who talked with his mouth full, interrupted others when they spoke, and couldn't use cutlery. Most importantly, when I was the main barman I could listen in and learn from, sometimes even interact with, senior worldly people. Knights and judges and surgeons and bankers. I saw how a series of regulars, judges and QCs fraternised with each other through jokes and ribbing and sometimes serious discussion. I had a long way to go, so I can't say the Auckland Club was a finishing school, but it sure helped a lot.

The next big learning curve, 'finishing school' if you like, was in law and law firms. If you want a guaranteed high calibre job in law, you want to be part of a big law firm summer clerk programme in your third year of law school. You can scrape together a job at the end of your law degree without this, but it is much more tenuous in terms of pay and ability to go anywhere in the law. Each big firm offers jobs to something like ten to thirty people. In my day, this was like eighty kids total out of many hundreds of law students around the country. The real sting in the tail was that, if you didn't get such a summer job, you would not get to clerk for the firm after your degrees were completed and you wouldn't have them paying for your post-degree bar admission course or keeping you on as a young lawyer. Conversely, if you were in for the summer clerking, you were in for law clerking and lawyering – almost invariably end of story, on your way to a brighter future.

This summer clerking process then really was a gatekeeping experience. I bet there aren't too many judges today, certainly High Court and above, who didn't work at one of these major firms at some point. Frankly, it's infinitely more difficult to be a quality lawyer without the mentoring and top-class training they provide. Summer clerking is also a ticket these days to working in a big firm in Australia, London and New York. Next to no one from New Zealand is going to get a job at Clifford Chance, a global law firm headquartered in London, if they haven't been at a Bell Gully, Chapman Tripp or two or three others. And if you summer clerk, you are on your way.

Off the back of my marks, I got interviews with most of the big firms, which was a big achievement. Then came the actual interviews, and it was like I was from Mars and the interviewers were from Venus. I didn't understand them and they didn't understand me. I remember leaving the interviews emotional, as I just didn't know what had happened. I've since learned that many students have interview coaches and study up on interview technique. More fundamentally, as I have indicated, most who get in are acculturated or steeped in the world of law beforehand. They have a dad, mum, granddad or uncle from the law, so understand what's going on. And from their family and schooling they have a confidence and a poise. Me, not so much.

I would have been as likely to get good advice from my parents about how to start a space start-up and launch rockets to the moon. So in I walked to Bell Gully and Russell McVeagh cold and unprepared. I couldn't answer the sort of things they asked, like a lamb to the inevitable slaughter. The rejection letters post-interview arrived in my letterbox in Te Atatū one by one. It seemed the game was over for me, and while those I'd befriended at law school were spending summers being wined and dined by firms trying to impress these best and brightest, I wasn't to be one of them. I was very low.

To make matters worse, my girlfriend at the time got accepted into every single firm. Like, every single bloody one. She was academically superior, and the fact she spoke fluent French, Italian, Spanish and German was, um, relatively impressive. But I believe in miracles and that God uses people around us to deliver them, and my girlfriend's mum was looking out for me. So when Kensington Swan contacted my girlfriend to understand why she'd said no to their summer clerkship, her mum suggested she put in a plug for me. She did and it worked. I hadn't even got an interview there initially, but they called and an interview was set up. This time my girlfriend and her mum prepped me; I now knew what to expect and had a pretty good sense of how I'd got the etiquette wrong before. Despite initial rejection, in the summer of 1998, I was a summer clerk at Kensington Swan.

The way it worked was that the clerk got rotated through the main teams within the firm. Pre-Christmas I was in the litigation department and after in the commercial team. In addition to learning the professional ropes, a clerk was expected to participate fully in the social life of the firm, and this for me was where trauma was coming.

As a young man from a teetotaler household I had limited, albeit growing, experience with alcohol. My attitude to it was juvenile. I struggled therefore at the Friday night drinks and other social events. In the late 90s these were still pretty raucous events at all the firms and frankly a real mixed message was sent. You were supposed to drink like a trooper but you couldn't make an ass of yourself. You can see where this is going.

One particular partner at the firm (now a Queen's Counsel), whom many of us young ones looked up to, was a Falstaffian-like character who would lead us astray, drinking and drinking and drinking. One Friday before Christmas, the drinking went on late into the evening, although sadly not late enough, as a fair few partners in the firm were still there. I was in a right state. Somehow I began a skolling competition of vodka shots with the partner, but not long in I couldn't hold it together. I power-chucked on an associate, a step or two away on the ladder from partnership, and was pretty embarrassed.

I soon forgot about this, but it was far from the end of the matter. On Monday that associate left me a drycleaning bill for his suit. Poor form, in my view, from a guy earning a lot of money, when what he should have done was pull me aside and give me a warning to take it easy at such events, because I was making a fool of myself, challenging partners to skolling competitions. Worse was to come. A week or so later, the head of HR called me into her office. She was a lovely woman and explained to me that the (junior) partner I was rotating to work under after Christmas saw my drinking escapade that Friday night and was refusing to have me on his team. This guy had classic new-partner syndrome, and in hindsight his was a real asshole's move. The HR manager explained this partner was pushing to ensure I was not offered a law clerking job the next year — which for reasons I've explained would be worse for me career-wise than had I never been offered the summer clerking role. Forever I would be known in New Zealand's relatively small legal community as the one guy who didn't get invited back. I was badly shaken up by this.

Fortunately, I was given a chance. The firm's senior partner and chair was prepared to have me work for him. I left work early after that HR meeting and when I came back the next day, I was a subdued young summer clerk who was maturing on the job very quickly. I basically stopped going to drinks functions and worked quietly and diligently for the older partner. He was a good guy and reasonably encouraging of me. Soon the summer clerking finished and I was back at university. A couple of months later, to my great relief, I received a letter from Kensington Swan inviting me to clerk the next summer.

One thing I can say about law firms is that no one ever made me feel stupid about my lack of elocution. At Kensington Swan, then later with Crown work, capability and work ethic got me a long way and also earned me the respect of my peers. I was a popular and respected lawyer, seen as going places. The accent mockery only started in politics. The worst came from, interestingly and surprisingly, more senior female journalists – who were fully paid-up life members of the liberal intelligentsia, the likes of Jane Bowron and Rosemary McLeod. There were others, too, who didn't seem to know how to write a column about me as leader without also discussing how I talked. They seemed obsessed by it. For some reason these comments really got to me, more than the huge buckets of shite I had poured over myself on relatively regular occasions about a bunch of other stuff. I think it was the personal nature of it: they were talking about me. Where I was from, what I was. I got much unsolicited advice and also some paid help, but I couldn't – and perhaps wouldn't – really shake how I talk.

As Natalie would say to me, in England at the BBC these days the regionalised accents are not only celebrated but practically mandated. The more working class and away from the posh 'received pronunciation', the higher in the Beeb you now go. To comment in any way negatively on this in the UK – well, good luck to you. You'd be safer picking a fight on Twitter over transgender issues. Changing how you speak is technically difficult but also, psychologically, I am resistant. It's who I am and change would feel like a betrayal of where and what I have come from. I am not Simon Bridges from Thorndon and never will be.

Elizabeth Gordon, a New Zealand language expert, in a piece for *The Spinoff*, put in writing what I wanted to say at the time, but couldn't find the words for. The various comments from media about my accent had really got to me, and I recall reading her column in an unguarded moment. It struck a nerve and I started crying. She argued that my accent makes clear that our country isn't classless as some like to believe, and after outlining the history and variations in pronunciation in our country she said:

> People make fun of Simon Bridges' pronunciation of English which has features of 'broad' NZ English. People who wouldn't dream of making jokes about a person's gender or ethnicity are very happy to make adverse comments or jokes about speakers using a lower class variety of language. It

doesn't matter that this is no more a matter of personal choice than the colour of the speakers' skin.[1]

To finish her piece, she quoted British expert Professor Peter Trudgill on me:

This is a fantastic New Zealand accent which I'm very excited to have heard, with many of the features which serve most strongly to distinguish the Kiwi from the Aussie. English-speaking people from the Northern Hemisphere generally have great trouble in telling Australians and New Zealanders from one another, but with Simon Bridges this is not the case. His is a very un-Australian accent with most of the innovating, modern NZ features which will over the coming decades take the two accents further apart.

The Kiwi accent is going to become more and more distinctive as the decades go by: all the accents of English around the world are gradually diverging from one another. Simon Bridges has an accent which is in many respects in the vanguard of this development in NZ. This is the accent of the New Zealand of the future, and people who don't like it had better get used to it.

I'm the new New Zealander, Rosemary McLeod. You better get used to it.

4
MASCULINITY

AS A KID I REMEMBER A CHAP, LET'S CALL HIM MERV, WHO WENT to Mum and Dad's church. Merv was a dumpy, thick-set sort of fellow who looked like his feet would smell or like he needed to shave a couple of times a day. Merv was *very* male, I would have thought. And indeed, Merv was married to a nice woman and they had kids. Then one day out of the blue Merv started coming to church as Mary, wearing frocks over her lorry-like body. She remained married and I suppose her wife and kids just went with it.

I don't remember what my father thought about this, but I do remember Mary coming to our home one day and she and Dad chatting. I imagine it put my father, as preacher, in something of a theological pickle, if that's not too inelegant a word to use, but I think my dad's answer was relatively enlightened for thirty-plus years ago: to continue loving the family and accepting them if they wanted to keep coming to church.

I also remember working at a great little café called Moka in Henderson for my old friends, the Corban family. Once every month or so a group of ladies came in for a huge slap-up dinner. They'd order hearty meals of lamb shanks, mash and chips and the like. What was so intriguing was that these ladies were in fact big blokes dressed as ladies. In the day they were all tradies, and happily heterosexually married over in South Auckland. But every so often their feminine sides came out. We called them Barbara and Sarah and Megan and so on, and made a real fuss of them.

Whether it's Merv, Barbara or Sarah, it seems to me in sex terms we know they are all men. As for their genders – well I probably need a PhD in the subject to make an informed comment. Me, I am a male. Never felt or had reason to believe otherwise. That's true for my sex and gender and everything else. I am also heterosexual, no doubt about that either. That said, I am more ambivalent about my masculinity or manliness. I feel we all have a masculine and feminine side, some more than others and in differing areas, and accentuated at different times in our lives.

In regards to masculinity, we all know there's a toxic side that comes in the form of bullying, sex and violence, and which probably manifests in other ways as well. This, thankfully, is a side of life that personally I haven't seen much of, at a direct family level at any event. So the reason I am personally unsure about my masculinity is because I don't live up to what I perceive is the Kiwi model of it. I haven't gone back to my university notes to revisit what Kiwi historian Jock Phillips, author of such quality tomes as *A Man's Country?*, says on this. Probably I don't need to. I only need to pick up a Barry Crump novel or a bestselling All Blacks memoir and it tells the story of an idealised stereotype.

Idealised masculinity in New Zealand is of the strong and laconic (possibly even silent) man. Think the late great Colin Meads or today Richie McCaw. Or in an arena other than rugby, Willie Apiata, Victoria Cross–decorated military hero. It's your physical, practical endeavours on the field that matter, and if you are asked about them afterward you'll perhaps have some difficulty describing them; you'd rather let your acts speak for themselves, to you they were nothing much.

Don't get me wrong. These humble men – and I have had the privilege of meeting all three – are outstanding individuals whose remarkable achievements *do* speak for themselves. They are also top blokes. Genuinely, better guys you couldn't meet. Yet you can see my difficulty and the difficulty of hundreds of thousands of other New Zealand men: these three men aren't us, not in the obvious ways or in less obvious ones.

In the most obvious sense, most men aren't Richie McCaw because we don't have his physical discipline, outstanding sporting prowess or leadership. But I'm more concerned with the highly accentuated characteristics of manliness in New Zealand that we emphasise through these gentlemen: physical (even if not at Richie's level), humble and laconic, to the point often of being horizontal. These are characteristics for men to emulate, even if you're a regular guy and not an elite operator like McCaw.

The physicality was always a difficulty for me. The role-modelling wasn't really there. While Dad loved watching sports from the armchair, he was a bit of a Māori Adrian Mole, for those of you who remember that teenage nerd book from some time back. I have no memory of any actual sporting interaction with Dad. No ball thrown or kicked, let alone him coming to watch my games from the sidelines; there were no such games. And the role modelling I did get wasn't great. I remember as a youngster one of my older brothers and me playing tennis at Rutherford High's courts one weekend. He was thirteen or fourteen years older than me, but kept berating me as a prepubescent boy for being 'unco' and unable to return the ball. That day his words sunk in and put me off team sports for the rest of my life. I was unco and not up to it. I never wanted to do that or feel that way again.

I don't mean to be hard on my old bro. Brotherly relationships aren't meant to be perfect and he unthinkingly just hit a nerve, stating the facts of the matter. I was maybe eight or nine, and I just hadn't developed hand-eye coordination. Dad hadn't invested in teaching it to me. Nor had my older brothers.

After that, it wasn't just sports that I never tried hard in. I also never tried in other practical activities that required physical, manly prowess and which I knew I would not be good at compared to others who'd had family members show them the way. The list includes fishing, boating and anything mechanical with my hands, whether tinkering, fixing or building. (I have sought to do some of these things more recently as my boys have wanted to.)

In reality, I doubt this 'unco' story that I remember is entirely true. It's not like I believe I would have made the All Blacks if Dad and my older brothers had practised with me every afternoon. But, while my hand-eye coordination for sports was underdeveloped, in other ways I had very good coordination and rhythm. In my teens and twenties I was a drummer in a cover band. Somehow there wasn't a mental block about my coordination when it came to musicality. I saw music and rhythm as things I could do. I'd loved music since I could hear. I remember using knitting needles to conduct orchestras to Mum's old LPs and listening again and again to my older brothers' record collections of 70s and 80s pop and rock when they weren't around, pretending I was Mick, Freddie or Elton.

And by not doing team sports I performed strongly in school, as I wasn't dividing my attention between the field and classroom. Economics 101 applied: being a jack of all trades can leave you master of none. Through channelling myself into school, I could smash the academic subjects and enjoy debating, music and shows. I didn't need to be an all-rounder and in fact maybe specialising made sense. I highlight this because, in New Zealand, if one isn't physically minded, there is a sense they are not much of a male. I caricature to an extent, but there is a truth in what I'm saying.

I'm also not saying how I think things should be but rather how, for many men, this is the perception. While we may not be hunting antelopes on the savannah anymore, we men are still judged on our physical prowess. Our pioneering society with more men than women was built on the likes of booze, physicality, rugby and sometimes war. Of course being active is great, but focusing on the physical neglects to recognise differences between men, and can be stereotyping and anti-intellectual.

Can I confess something? I prefer reading history to watching rugby. Sure, I enjoy going along to big internationals or watching them on TV with my kids. The ritualistic nature of the anthems and then the haka, and the athleticism and skill displayed by the players are great. I get it and don't begrudge many Kiwis their love of rugby. But I have never once in my life intentionally watched a non-international game such as Super Rugby alone. It just doesn't float my boat. I'd rather finish a book on pre-Leninist Russia.

To those of you reading this from overseas (all four of you), let me explain that this is a courageous thing for a male politician in New Zealand to say. I can see John Key shaking his head in disbelief, now more sure than ever why he backs Chris Luxon and Nicola Willis. Being an atheist or gay in New Zealand is no longer any sort of big deal, but what I have just said is, to many, an automatic disqualification from leading our country (hence my saying it now). I actually do think it takes some courage for a Kiwi man to say rugby doesn't matter much to him, and it's also probably very bad for book sales. But I'd bet there are many more like me than is commonly thought. New New Zealanders, as well as a bunch of others, just aren't as massively into it.

What this means for me in a practical sense as a politician is that in many chats with All Blacks, coaches and business heads at games and parties, I feign interest. That's not a terrible thing. For example, I have empathy for people who are intimidated by politics just like I am with rugby, where they don't follow it enough to confidently talk about it. That said, we should all tell the truth. And so I am, right here, right now. Just as I don't need to speak te reo to be Māori, I don't need to love rugby to be a Kiwi male. Really, truly, I actually don't.

I also still can't back a boat or build a deck. Again, for those of you reading this offshore, please recognise the courage in this statement made from Tauranga, New Zealand. One of my good mates is a salt-of-the-earth builder. We share walks up the Mount and laughs over a couple of beers. But he certainly takes the piss out of me that I can't back his tinny into the Sulphur Point boat ramps for him. He says he finds it hard to vote for a guy who can't. Of course he's joking, but in reality I know he finds it hard to fathom. To him, men fish and boat and build. But Dad didn't (to be fair, once a year at Christmas he'd go out by himself on a fishing charter for a day – though the only thing I remember him catching is his finger one year, and Mum took him to the doctor). And so nor did I growing up, and only recently through 'real men' like my mate have I gone out fishing on the ocean and round the beautiful Rotorua lakes.

These are big admissions for me. Another mate once said to me that the meaning of life in Tauranga (and probably much of New Zealand) is owning a Ford Ranger and a boat. I represent all this as a Member of Parliament, these good men and their values, as best I can. But I am different.

At its worst and extreme, an emphasis on male physicality is so toxic that for some men, it encourages sexual and physical violence. I am not talking rugby anymore. I am saying that, more broadly, the idea men have to be big and physical can be a real problem. I got beaten up a number of times growing up in Te Atatū North. At intermediate school when wrestling was all the rage, the kids who already had bodies like adults used to practise their triple suplexes on me. It made me scared to go to school for a time. Biking everywhere at that age, I knew the streets down which to bike extra fast because if I went too slowly I'd be asking for trouble.

At high school we all started going to parties. I remember a couple where somewhere, somehow, the punches were being put on me. And I was a lover, not a fighter. A real easy target. Dad didn't teach ball and he didn't teach fighting either. I also have memories of one party where a couple of guys in my class, drunk, turned on me for no reason. In seeking to beat me up, as I tried to get away, they ripped my shirt off. I ran and walked home through the streets of West Auckland that night without a top on.

Sometimes it was my mouth that got me into trouble, but oftentimes it was just a wrong time and place. There sadly was, and I suspect is, a level of violence that goes with the territory in certain places in New Zealand. At the end of sixth form, I somehow was scooting about in a mini with a young guy a year or two below me and some others. His older brother was loosely a mate and in my year group. He can't have had his licence for long. There were a few of us; I don't recall what we were doing or where we were going. But the kid lost control on Te Atatū Road and the car went careening through a brick wall. I remember this bit well, despite the fact it's nearly thirty years ago. Things went into slow motion as we drove into the bricks, impacted and then came out the other side to a stop in someone's front yard. I had never been in a car accident of any description before and I freaked out. I was in shock. I got out of the car and ran home as fast as my legs would carry me.

Later that night, around eleven I reckon, I got a call from the older brother in my year, not a bad sort of a guy. He was angry I had left his brother at the scene and was calling me from outside my house. He wanted me to come outside. In all honesty he made a good point. I don't know why I did a runner; I had been shocked and scared. And while the younger brother was okay, I should have stuck around. I went outside and there he was, on the driveway next to us which led down to the Baptist Church. He asked me to take my glasses off – I was shortsighted in those days – and I did. He then smacked me in the face. I can't recall how many times, but I felt my left jaw crack. I was guzzling blood down my throat. He got in his car and left. I felt scared and alone. My parents were asleep in bed and I was outside our family home. I was ashamed and embarrassed, and didn't want to wake them. But I knew it was serious, my jaw was wobbling about, no longer straight and still like a soldier, and the blood was flowing, as if it were a river flooding its banks.

I telephoned the best friend of my closest brother, Mark, six years older than me. I must have slipped inside quietly to do this. I am unsure where Mark was, as I would probably have sought him out were he home. All my other siblings had left home by my high school years. Mark's mate John was at university and lived not far away. We'd been through some hard times together so I knew he would empathise. He biked around from the other side of the suburb and, after a chat, it was clear I needed to go to A&E. His ten-speed wouldn't get me there, and the olds would have to find out at some point.

I was in at Middlemore for a few days and had my first ever surgery, next to a gang member who'd fallen off his motorbike and whose girlfriend kept coming in and shagging him behind the curtains of his bed. My surgery involved a titanium plate that I still have in my jaw. Dad was insistent I complain to the police. I wanted it all to go away, but Dad's view was right and won out in the end. Police prosecuted and, while I don't recall the sentence, I recall being given $500 victim reparations, which seemed a lot of money as a teenager. I remember telling the victims' advisor about being scared going out in the streets at night after this, but in Te Atatū you really didn't have a choice. Fortunately kids are forgiving. School had broken for the year and, when we started back again, everyone moved on. I was head boy (pinnacle of my career) and it was a good year.

I don't tell any of this to say 'woe is me'. Nor am I saying this unsporty kid who was beat up all the time was a down-on-his-luck loser growing up. No way. I had no shortage of friends and enjoyed life in the West. I was a popular, hardworking but fun-loving kid. But in my teen years, I suppose I was learning intuitively what I now also know to be true: aspects of our Kiwi culture idolise the physical in males in an unhealthy way. Since Adam was a cowboy, crime and victimisation stats have shown how appallingly unsafe it is to be a young man in New Zealand. You shouldn't need to be good with your fists to grow up male in our country.

Additionally, according to the mythmakers, great Kiwi men are humble. This is, normally speaking, an incredibly good quality and is more often than not an endearing one among Kiwis generally. But the 'It was nothing much' response after winning the World Cup or climbing Everest often isn't actually true. The achievement *is* something much! Americans and our brasher Aussies are somewhat right to say so when they achieve big. They seem to have a healthier regard for themselves.

I would never want to be a Yank or an Aussie. They can be too much. But humility that shades into dishonest lack of regard for what we are capable of and what we have achieved (or even worse, self-loathing) can have negative consequences for individuals, turning up as a lack of self-worth and belief, or on the world stage as a cultural cringe.

As my wife, with her PR business, likes to say: you can't sell a secret. I've often, from my Christian upbringing, hoped that hard work and excellence shine through in the end. But often they don't. Jim or Jenny, who tell everyone everything about the single good thing they did, get the payrise. I've learned that a squeaky wheel gets the oil.

Collectively as a nation, do we allow ourselves to be intimidated in the international arena out of a false humility? Is the fact that we need visiting foreigners to praise New Zealand as the friendliest, or most beautiful or kindest, not a mirror image of our 'humility', a self-doubt we collectively share as a nation? We are a great nation, and should be loud and proud on the world stage. It's in our self-interest to do so.

The laconism of New Zealand men is also an indisputable fact. This isn't just a sporting thing. It exists across all class distinctions, from pig hunter to private gentleman's club. My barman experience at the Auckland Club taught me a lot about how businessmen interact. I learned how successful men joke and rib and talk seriously with each other. First and foremost, such chats are steeped in euphemism and not saying too much. Whereas other cultures will bluntly call a spade a shovel and describe it intimately, we tend to say, 'Yep, it does the job,' and leave it at that.

I don't see this as at all similar to the stiff British upper lip or reserve. That seems to me a more intentional and judgemental thing, saying little as if from pride. For us, it's perhaps unconsciously motivated by the opposite desire: not being overbearing or thinking ourselves better than those we are with, a false humility if you will. To over-describe the spade would be full of ourselves.

Taken together, the emphasis on physicality, humility and not being full of ourselves may also be a part of our mental health and suicide downfall. If a man asks a man what's wrong he says, 'Yeah nah, I'll be okay.' John Kirwan has been a brilliant leader in this domain but let's never be complacent. Being humble and laconic protects one from that Kiwi bommy knocker, the tall poppy phenomenon. But it's not only the high achieving who are knocked down. We also knock difference in New Zealand.

In recent decades great work has been done to embrace certain diversities and break down stigmas in our country. And yet, are New Zealanders really as tolerant as we think we are? Britain has different bigotries, but I hugely admire the freedom to be eccentric in the UK. Natalie went to school in Coventry with a chap called Daniel Lismore. He takes, I suppose, the dandy tradition and adds nuclear fission to it. Today he has a massive UK following enthralled by his make-up and regalia, and you can check him out on Instagram where he describes himself as a living sculpture. I wonder how he would get on in Whangarei or for that matter Auckland? In New Zealand we are much more homogeneous, blue top milk, than we think. I recently saw a book on English eccentrics, and they are celebrated there. Where are ours, I wonder? I don't see many.

Today we seek more women in non-traditionally feminine trades and workspaces. In my old profession of law, where once women weren't even allowed, female law graduates are now in the majority, albeit with a way to go in terms of other more significant professional benchmarks like partnerships and on the Bench. So I can't really make an apples for apples comparison between men and women. Traditionally female roles in the workforce still earn less than the traditionally male. But culturally, as we seek to knock over stereotypes and break down barriers for women, let's also try a bit harder to do likewise for men. I am not male by virtue of how much beer I drink, how built I am, nor by a bunch of other traditional yardsticks, or yard glasses for that matter. Don't typecast me.

As I have never met the Kiwi masculine ideal in so many ways, I've looked to fulfil it in other ways. A primary one has been work. I am sure there are female workaholics – for me, it has been part of my identity and I think my masculinity. I grew up in an old-fashioned nuclear family. Not radioactive, but one with a dad, one mum and some siblings. I believe we were very blessed as children because every day when we came home from school, Mum, as a stay-at-home mother, was there for us. I know Natalie would poke her eyes out with sticks if she had to be a full-time 'homemaker', but people are different and I also know my mother loved it. She reluctantly went back to work as a primary school teacher when I was in my teens, only because my parents needed the money for a house deposit after years in a church house.

Of course, the past is the past. I am not advocating for stay-at-home mums in a fit of US-style moral conservative nostalgia. Today, both sexes overwhelmingly work in paid employment even if women still probably have the much harder job with the 'struggle of the juggle' of home and work – women still do more than men at home despite both working, not counting a growing minority of stay-at-home dads. What I am saying is that, as a child, my role-modelling was of a distant man at work and a loving mum at home. If I am really honest, deep, deep down, being a man has always, to me, meant being the breadwinner. I appreciate how ridiculous this is and I am ashamed to even say it out loud. But what's hardwired can be hard to reprogramme.

Being the breadwinner is not even a reality for me. I don't complain about my paypacket from the Kiwi taxpayer as a backbench MP; I know it's much more than what the average New Zealander earns. In recent times, though, Natalie has made significantly more than me through her PR business. She pays most of the bills, and I'm grateful. The wine I drink is much better because of her. Yet thousands of years ago I would be out in the savannah throwing a spear at an animal. Me male, me provide for you. Ugh-a-ugh-a.

Natalie's transition to being the dominant breadwinner has been slow. When we had our first child, Emlyn, it became too hard for her to work from nine till five, or seven in her case. Working for yourself allows flexibility and autonomy, even if that comes at a cost of stress and responsibility. I encouraged her to start her own business and backed her to succeed. These days she has several top staff and a great list of valued clients.

Honestly, I wouldn't have been mature enough to handle her success earlier in life. I know this because a long time ago I had a girlfriend in another profession who was more successful than me. Earned more, better car, more status. I didn't like it, couldn't handle it, and it was a factor in our split. Honestly, I know that how I used to feel isn't rational or right; it's the hunter-gatherer thing that's taken me time to be a better, real man about. Today, Natalie says I am a great feminist. I believe in her and want our Jemima to be a world-beater too, as I know she has that potential. We all grow and develop, and I am secure enough in myself today to not be such a fool as I once was. But while I am now well and truly over the breadwinner complex, my workaholism has been harder to shake. It's a strong part of my masculine identity.

Dad's life has been defined through his work and so has mine. Add in the Protestant ethic and I find it very difficult not to work. Isn't it what men do? Many men may not have this hang-up but I suspect a fair few do. Slowly I am improving. Losing the leadership of the National Party helped a lot. I discovered that my male identity wasn't simply through work; much more it's through being a loving husband and father. But I must keep reminding myself of this. Incidentally, that means I now enjoy watching a bit more rugby, going outdoors to fish and there is even talk of some hunting. It's all for my boys – not to ensure they meet some stereotype, but because they ask for it and love it.

This chapter probably demonstrates that working through the question of what makes a real man isn't easy for me, or for a lot of men. Part of the answer lies in Kiwis being more accepting of difference in less obvious ways than, say, acceptance of sexuality or one's mental health. Men aren't all All Blacks, strong silent types. We aren't all hundred-hour week high-paid workers either. A stay-at-home dad looking after his kids ... he's a real man too.

5
MARRIAGE

OUR EXAMS HAD JUST FINISHED. AND ON 18 JULY 2005, A SHOWERY Oxford summer's day, Natalie and I got married at St Cross Chapel, a beautiful little stone church built a thousand years ago and around the corner from the university college where I lived and we met.

Natalie, twenty-two, wore a golden cocktail dress as we couldn't afford a proper wedding one. And me? I was twenty-eight and in an old work suit. The congregation was a bit rent-a-crowd when I look back at it. Lots of international students from Russia, Brazil, India, Greece and everywhere else, with whom we drank and laughed that year but have never seen since. A sister and brother of mine had made the trip to be there, as had a few Kiwi friends of mine from London. Natalie had a smattering of friends and family.

After the wedding we shouted everyone drinks at our

college common room then a small group of us went to a lovely little restaurant in a Victorian glasshouse, where early in our relationship I had splashed out to impress Natalie with New Zealand sauvignon blanc. I'd cried poor on the wedding and reception, and it was all paid for by my mum and dad for a couple of grand. Then we were back to Natalie's parents' that evening. What a way to spend the first marital night! Days after that, we got on separate planes back to New Zealand via a 'honeymoon' in Hong Kong. My round-the-world return ticket, purchased before I'd even left New Zealand a bit over a year back, already had me stopping there, and the plane was full so we bought another for Natalie.

At her tender age she had never been in the southern hemisphere. Heck, she hadn't even seen much of the UK. The Asian heat hit her hard, as did the culture shock of not being in the north. When we finally arrived in Mount Maunganui on the evening of the last day of July, her first impression in the dark was of port lights and an industrialised wasteland. I think she wondered if she'd made a mistake. Natalie of course is half-Polish, and David Lange had rightly been disparaging about Polish shipyards a while back. Well, she felt she was back at them and that they were even worse, given she was now in the middle of nowhere on the other side of the world. This certainly wasn't the picture postcard I had sold to her.

Well, the sun came up the next morning and Mount Maunganui beach was beautiful. Maybe it would be okay.

Maybe. We were a couple of streets back from the beach at my folks' place, bought when Dad's older sister, Aunty Lorna, passed and they inherited. They were still living in Auckland at that time. We could survive okay on cheap rent and just my lawyer's salary, but Natalie wasn't having that and got a job at the *Bay of Plenty Times* as a young reporter doing death-knocks and seeking out frontpage stories. It wasn't the BBC, where she had interned as a youngster, but it was something in Tauranga and a good training in print journalism from the old salties who still worked in regionals back then.

I am in awe of what she did, travelling with me and leaving the closeknit family I had ripped her from. It was all very traditional: marriage, travelling around the world with your man into the unknown. We hadn't even lived together before in our year-long relationship, as I'd been in college and she'd been flatting. This caused problems when Immigration New Zealand in London wanted proof ours was a real marriage. I had to end up getting angry at them to get her back home.

But we got married because we were in love, and I wanted to show Natalie I was serious about her moving with me across the world. I wasn't a fly-by-night used-car salesman who'd leave her in the lurch. And my religious parents, who'd be subsidising the rent, wouldn't want that either. The miracle is that her parents went with it. To put it gently, I'm not sure how keen they were on me. Then again, I suppose they couldn't talk: as a much older British man, Natalie's dad had brought home to the Midlands a young lass he met at a trade show in Poznan, Poland.

Getting married these days seems to be less and less popular. Or rather, living together in relationships without marriage has over time become more popular. Legally, I am not sure it matters too much anymore. After a couple of years, the presumption is that half of what's yours is theirs and vice versa, regardless of a marriage certificate – that is whether there was a marriage, a civil union (which the bush lawyer in me thinks is for all intents and purposes the same as marriage), or just living together as de factos in the nature of old-style marriage. The little joke about wedding rings being the world's smallest handcuff isn't true anymore. Once you hit a point on the timeline you're chained up and in just as deep, with or without the wedding band.

And that's before we even get to the D word, no longer the taboo it once was. As a young lawyer I recall chats with older lawyers about their court cases seeking to prove the grounds for divorce. They literally had private investigators out snooping around, trying to catch hubby in the act of coitus with some scarlet woman around the corner from the marital home. 'And as I sat in my car across the road, I saw the lights go off in her bedroom, your Honour. Then in the shadows against drawn blinds, I saw movements up and down, up and down, consistent with the act of sexual intercourse. Not long after, Mr Brown left the house in a hurry.'

Today, separation and divorce are as easy as one-two-three, and are the outcome of roughly four in ten marriages. I'm not going to get all sentimental, but I do find the decline of marriage and rise of divorce sad. Marriage is a signifier of commitment. Yep, I get and accept that people can be just as committed in other ways. Marriage is still a culturally significant way, though. It's an institution in which people show their commitment to each other and often together to their children. That stability is a real security for kids growing up, provided the marriage is a happy one.

In that regard, the commitment of marriage is actually a lot like having kids. Both situations are pretty easy to get into, then hard but satisfying and worth fighting for. For me, marriage – like kids – has been a refining process. I am a selfish guy with a thousand life goals – career and personal. Marriage and kids have reminded me and kept me grounded in the needs and aspirations of those around me, and have kept me outward-focused when I could so easily have turned inwards.

Fact is, there are times when I would probably enjoy a few more drinks with mates on an evening out. But I know Jemima and Harry will need a little help early the morning after, and that keeps me on the straight and narrow. Thankfully neither wakes in the night anymore and, for all Natalie does for them, it's the least I can do to be up making a bottle and some food at six or seven in the morning. Going with Emlyn to some of his sports and community involvements forces me to not only hang with him, but also to see what's really happening in our community among mixed demographic groups. Because of Natalie, Emlyn, Harry and Jemima, I am not an island.

I sometimes joke to Natalie that, were I an island – divorced from her – how different things would be. I would be living in a spartan apartment with one chair, a TV, a set of cutlery and maybe one pot plant if I was lucky. All the creature comforts and the family accoutrements, from the art and the cushions to the half-drunk milk bottles and half-chewed dog toys, would be gone. Sure, it would be efficient, and I would wake up in the morning with the freedom to do whatever my type-A personality wants. But it wouldn't really be living, not how I have done in my family with its little community of kids' friends, friends' parents, babysitters and their stories and so on. Not only would the big D be bad for my kids, and I hope from her perspective for Natalie, it would be a Titanic-like disaster for me.

People often ask me about parliament and how tough it must be on a relationship. Natalie and I were married before I became an MP and didn't have children at the start – for seven years, in fact. My perception is that parliament can be tough on relationships in a couple of respects. For most MPs, we aren't home during the week as we're away in Wellington. And even when parliament isn't on, MPs need to be away from home a lot and out many nights by professional necessity. Just the time away, in and of itself, strains a marriage week after week, month after month, year after year. When you add the emotional toll from this, it can be even worse. Some can't take it.

Secondly, the life of an MP involves booze. At parliament, there's a lot of it around. It's a social lubricant and, as you seek to get on with colleagues and just get on politically, that makes you susceptible to tiredness and can add strain to a marriage. Not only are you away but, when you get back home, you're knackered. A partner then wants to go out and paint the town red, but I suspect for most MPs after a week in the House – up late with colleagues, sometimes drinking – what we want is just a cup of tea and a lie down.

As a wise senior MP said to me as a newbie, if your marriage was rocky before you got to parliament, you're in trouble. But if it was good, you should be fine. (He also said, regarding having kids, that there are only two ways to do it vis-à-vis parliament: wait till their teens before you stand, or have 'em when you're there so they know no different. But I digress.)

Personally I am grateful I met Natalie before I became an MP. Standing for parliament was an exciting shared experience for us as young people, pre-kids – when we could enjoy it purely and, dare I say, somewhat smugly. As I have progressed and the grey hairs have started to accumulate, I am grateful also to be hitched. Parliament can be a lonely place, and my phone calls with Natalie, sometimes many times in an hour but at least several a day, have been a huge moral support for me. We usually just ring to touch base and check in. Sometimes to bitch (never about my own colleagues, you understand!) or share a victory. Sometimes one of us needs advice on how to deal with a thorny issue or prickly customer.

I feel for MPs who come to parliament without a partner or who separate while they are there, and therefore who don't have the friendship and support like what I've had from Natalie. She's been there for me at my triumphs and helped me at the toughest times. When I won the leadership of National, Natalie was there in parliament right beside me and also again when I lost it two-and-a-bit years later. Funnily enough, I also called her down to Wellington a couple of other times when I'd felt like a spill against me might be on, although they didn't on those occasions eventuate.

Some MPs make the decision to keep their partner away. That works for them both. But for Natalie and me, it's been a complete partnership the whole time, probably because we started the adventure together so young. We've lived in and out of each other's pockets and relied on each other to get through.

While it can be tough and unique, I am not sure the life of an MP is massively worse for a relationship than a bunch of other stressful jobs out there. In recent times there has been media talk about the bed-hopping. While it undoubtedly happens, I think it's again not too much worse than other workplaces. If you're looking for it, you'll find it. If you're not, you won't. Throughout my time at parliament there have been many rumours of shagging among colleagues, among staff, among press, by MPs in other parties, and even every so often by MPs cross-party. Yes, there is fuel for this in the pressure and stress, the time away from family, combined with the hours and booze. But more often than not and as much as I can tell, the rumours have proven untrue.

Remember also the big downsides to playing away. It's true, there has long been an unwritten rule among media and politicians that consensual activity among adults, say MPs, should be private. But on occasion, it hasn't taken too much for the convention to fall away. In an age of smartphones and social media and, quite rightly, a focus on power imbalances as well as outright harassment and abuse, there is a lot for a politician to lose. Fortunately the rumours have never been about me. I've steered well clear of extra-curricular activity.

Anyhow, I like the Biblical conception of marriage. At its essence, it's that two become one. Of course that's not physically true. Wills and Kate, George and Mildred, Simon and Natalie – we are different sentient beings. But aren't spouses a bit like pet owners who look like their pet? This does happen in marriage over time, I believe, whether because couples end up eating, dressing and living the same, and thus looking the same, or for some other mysterious reason I can't quite fathom. Metaphysically, to an extent my experience has followed the Lord's instruction in the first book of the Bible that Adam and Eve become one person. It hasn't been an overnight thing, over years of give and take, getting it wrong then trying to make it right, sharing and growing, laughing and crying, Natalie and I have had a profound effect on each other, changing one another and becoming so similar that we sometimes know what each is thinking before words are said.

It's taken me several years, for example, to work out how angry Natalie will be if I take the kids on an outdoor adventure without sunscreen on. So now, after years of seeing the anger, I actually apply sunscreen to them. Funnily enough, the kids don't get as burned as they used to. Natalie has also worked out, over nearly two decades, that buying new house furniture every couple of months isn't always necessary and tends to wind me up. Consultation is necessary, because houses *can* have too many couches and cushions.

Significantly, I have made Natalie more rightwing (she's possibly more rightwing than me now) and she's made me more leftwing. Thanks to me, Natalie does more physical activity – walking and biking up and down mountains.

Thanks to her, I enjoy more visual arts – fashion, even gardening magazines. The simple point is, we have rubbed off on each other over time.

Now, some won't like this idea and fair enough. We live in an age of independence and individuality and autonomy, and I love that. 'I shouldn't have to change' or 'I value my autonomy', you say. My rejoinder would be that that's okay on the minor stuff: just because my wife likes hip hop, I don't have to. I am not suggesting one should allow their personality to be subsumed by the other's. But overall, if a couple isn't changing and growing together, then call me old fashioned but they're probably growing apart. That could mean Harry has to sell his boat to split its proceeds with Meghan, and Fergie will need to likewise with her jewellery. That's before we even consider the bigger costs when a couple with kids separate, like loneliness and inner turmoil.

My experience of marriage is that it has made me a better person. 'You must have been a terrible person beforehand,' I hear you say. Well, yes and no. Natalie, too, is a better person, and it goes both ways. For example, Natalie comes from a family where if you have money, you spend it. I come from a family where if you have money, you don't. Over a long time we've both realised neither side has it quite right. You can't live all for today, as that creates too much uncertainty tomorrow, but living all for tomorrow is flinty and boring. Natalie still has more Trelise Cooper and Zambesi than I feel she strictly needs, but these days I enjoy living a little as well. I can enjoy meat that isn't mince and luncheon sausage, and when I eat out in great restaurants I'm less obsessed with price. Natalie has learned some Tory fiscal prudence while I've adopted a bit more life in my life.

I've mentioned luncheon sausage, which is now banned in our house (fortunately Natalie still allows me a kid's cocktail sausage once in a while), but food has been another area of dispute. In my household we never had enough. Despite my family experiencing greater prosperity in recent years, where no one is short of a bob, the mentality has tended to continue, with Bridges family events sometimes ending without enough food. After all, you don't want to waste it, so don't cook too many potatoes or chickens or turkey. In Natalie's family there will be potatoes prepared eight ways, and so many of them that half will be thrown out. Meat – we need it all, they'll say. Chicken, turkey, pork, beef and more. Again, Natalie and I have met in the middle. I see the error in my family's ways and she now recognises we don't need to prepare for forty people if only ten are coming.

So, yes, another difference is our families. Natalie's is close, to the point of FaceTime on the toilet and a need for contact daily from the UK. If one person needs something from the supermarket, everyone must go and discuss which brand of baked beans is best. My family is very, shall we say, utilitarian. Visits to see each other are rationed because you can have too much of a good thing. Again, now Natalie and I meet in the middle: I like family being closer but we agree that her mum and sister don't need to be with us on FaceTime all day!

Natalie's family has always emphasised cleanliness. Their family home is dusted and sanitised within an inch of its life, and yet the ironing board is irritatingly always out in the living room with unironed clothes. In my family home, it's the opposite. Today though, for Natalie, I am more hygiene-conscious and Natalie is tidier. We have become more similar, if not the same.

To me, then, marriage is a partnership worth fighting for. Yep, you'll need a bit of negotiation and give-and-take, and you'll change and grow and be better for it. You'll find friendship and support and love.

I should re-emphasise friendship. Natalie and I have a lot of laughs and this keeps us happy together. I am not exactly a prankster but I do have the odd – in every sense of the word – recurring prank on my wife. Natalie complains she never sees me sleeping. That's not quite true, but I do tend to be up in the morning before her. I am a morning person and she's … not. I am also sometimes a restless sleeper through the night. So over the years, when I am awake and she's not, I have taken to doing a little amateur photography and videography of her sleeping. You see, my wife, against all evidence, believes that she doesn't sleep with her mouth wide open. My file of photos titled Natalie Mouth Open, taken over many years, shows that she certainly does. I took the first one on our honeymoon in Hong Kong. The poor petal was pooped from the travel and heat. And from there the file just grew and grew. In addition, it's a commonly known fact that women don't snore. I accept this – it would be impolite not to. Some do breathe rather heavily though, and some even from time to time growl. Like my file of photos, my video collection bears witness to the facts.

Natalie and the kids also have their little jokes on me. Those are harder to explain but often they are recurring in-jokes against me. For example, for a long time they've all insisted there is a shortcut from our house to my parents' place at the Mount over the other side of town. I've now proved many a time that this isn't the case, but *every* blinkin' trip they enjoy relitigating this and winding me up.

The jokes have been needed because marriage hasn't always been plain sailing. I am ultimately an introvert, as I discuss later, while Natalie is an extroverted people-person. Opposites do attract, but they don't always gel perfectly. The biggest source of misunderstandings has been these characteristics at the centre of our personalities, where I have oftentimes sought to withdraw from company and been under-responsive to Natalie, and she hasn't understood what this means. Likewise in the past I've been perplexed by her desire for people all around us or for endless 'communication' when I've felt we've said all that needs to be said about what's going on at work or with family. Over time, we've both met each other's needs with give and take, and also understood each other better. Thank God it hasn't taken professional counselling!

Finally, for marriage to work, you need to decide, sometimes even daily, that you want it to. Recently my family went to the traditional Indian wedding of our good friends' daughter. It was wonderful. We went for a full day, but the wedding celebration had already gone on for two or three days before that with another day or two to follow. There were beautiful flowers, colourful saris, confetti, samosas, even ornate swords, everywhere. The wedding couple's marriage was arranged, and I should be clear this is very different from a forced one. As I understand it, the parents think deeply and make a preliminary selection based on their assessment of the couple's suitability. Then the putative bride and groom meet and they decide if there is chemistry. If there is, well, it is all on.

At first blush, the thought of this makes Westerners very uneasy I am sure. Parents and wider family shouldn't have any decision rights over a marriage. We in the West believe in romantic love and that there is 'the one' for us somewhere. Frankly, if it had been left to mine and Natalie's parents, we would never have been married. I don't think either side entirely approved! But I am told arranged marriages are much more successful and go the distance at much higher rates than our Western versions, so maybe, just maybe, we don't know everything.

I can see why arranged marriages hold better over a long time. Love is a feeling, but if you are relying on ongoing infatuation to keep you in a marriage five, ten, twenty-five years down the line, you've no chance. Marriage is a decision. Whether Western or culturally arranged, marriage requires a choice, an ongoing decision and commitment to make it work. If it's just good ol' Hollywood romance, like in the movies, that keeps you in it – well, the D day is coming. If it's a decision to make it work for yourselves but also your families and your values, I suspect it must endure longer and stronger and actually happier. I am certainly not making a case for sticking in a bad marriage. Just, I suppose, for a sense that if you do one day sign the dotted line, you decide to commit to growing together. There are bad times in every marriage, but if you can get through them, you become closer.

Today, statistically, the happiest people are older. Your seventies are meant to be your happiest decade, and this stands to reason if you've got your health and a bit of cash. You're not trying to prove anything, you've worked things out, and life can be good. I am sure this basic point is also true the longer you're married.

I know it's true for my parents. Their marriage hasn't always been perfect, especially through times of making ends meet for six hungry kids under one roof. But then things got better. They mellowed and understood each other – not fully, but more than in the past. In the marathon of marriage, the second half can be the best.

6
FATHERHOOD

WHEN MY FATHER HELD MY HAND WHEN I WAS A YOUNG CHILD and we crossed the road together, my cheeks would grow hot and my eyes would well up. I felt confused and embarrassed because his physical touch was so uncommon.

For Dad to be holding my hand meant Mum was somehow unable to and that he was there with us, out and about, both of which were not usual. Physically, my dad is a large man. Six-foot-two. The recurring joke for my mum was that, when she married him, she got 'tall, dark … well, two out of three isn't bad.' And he was ungainly or awkward in his general movement, albeit meticulous and particular with his hands, like when he picked a hot chip out of newspaper wrapping or when he was writing something.

Today he is a bit like a tortoise or tuatara. He rarely moves, but when he does it's very deliberate and slow. Yet the awkwardness has increased and, when combined with his stiffness – he's like a plank – it means he's a hazard, often bruising himself or worse, tripping and doing real damage. The hands have become shaky, perhaps with undiagnosed Parkinson's to go with his dementia.

Emotionally, as I was growing up, my father was an island. Like one of those islets I know so well out from the Mount beach. You could in theory swim across to it and visit, but for some reason you never do. Dad was just like that. Always present but distant.

While Mum was all cuddles and love, moments of physical contact with my father could be counted on one hand. Today, as he is in his late eighties, I will sometimes put my hand on his shoulder or head jokingly, but a hug is a Rubicon I do not cross.

It was more than the lack of physical contact. There was little connection there in other ways. I remember scrunching up teacher's notes and hiding the fact of parent–teacher interviews from my parents. I can't recall exactly why I didn't want my parents there, but I think it was a complex mix of sparing Mum the trouble (she was a super-mum singlehandedly raising six kids) and also knowledge that Dad wouldn't come. He didn't come to anything. Probably other dads did, but mine didn't.

As for school sports, where today parents are expected to drive all over town to take little Johnny to football and

Emma to ballet, I have no recollection of Dad and I ever doing anything sporting together. We never once threw or kicked a ball, let alone had him come to a game. There were no games. In contrast, my kids run us ragged with ballet, hockey, St Johns, rock climbing, tennis, the list goes on.

There were six of us kids in the Bridges household, eight in total under one roof. We wouldn't really engage with Dad during the day. He was there doing his thing and we were there doing ours. There would possibly be a skirmish over food – say, a biscuit or the last sausage – and that would be the size of it. But there was one strange way Dad would 'connect' with all of us from time to time. When we had gone to bed, he would come into the room, turn the light on and look at us. Mostly he would just look, but every so often he would sniff the back of our heads in the hair – something I now do to my children, as it's a smell I love. If we complained about the light being on and being woken up, he would say something along the lines of 'Shut up or I will thump you,' (which he never did). Then he would turn the light off and leave.

Like I say, he was always present – or at least *a* presence – even if not emotionally or relationally; watching TV as we all would in the lounge, on the couch or the floor. Dad was religious about religion and TV. The 6 pm news must be watched. And sports. Sometimes in the summer this would be in his singlet and Y-fronts. Looking back, he did all he knew and all he could. He had no 'love language' from his own upbringing and was somewhat emotionally retarded. At least he came in at nights for the look or the sniff.

If it wasn't dinner time or all of us in front of the goggle box, my memory is that Dad would be in his study down in the garage, adjoining the church carpark. The garage was a small double made of steel. At the end, he had a separated lockable office filled with books and cassette tapes on shelves. In some ways it was not dissimilar to a professor's office, though spartan, with no leather or sherry. It was plain and simple, drab even, but functional. In this room Dad would read and, I presume, pray and listen to tapes from gospel preachers from around the world so he could draw inspiration for his sermon that Sunday. The tapes came in elaborate packaging from global mega-ministries and cost a fortune from his own pocket. As for the sermons, he wrote those out in his particular, peculiar, blockprint-capitals handwriting on lined paper. Dad sought opportunities to preach anywhere and everywhere. He loved the performative, persuasive and cerebral aspects of it. Preaching gave him identity; eventually I would bring the same approach to my jury trial work. The preparation was its own meditation and every bit as important as the delivery. After Dad delivered his sermons he stored them in this office, each one tied together with brown string he cut and pulled together in the fastidious way he did everything with his hands. This office and those sermons were his professional and vocational life. When he reluctantly retired, the garage and this study were so full of Christian and theological books, tapes and sermons that Mum insisted he sell them before we moved from the manse into our first ever home of our own, this time in Te Atatū South, not North. Such was his collection that he raised many, many thousands of dollars.

I can't remember much about my dad growing up. If you don't swim out to the island, the memories aren't that strong. But by all accounts he was a powerful preacher: in its hey-day of Holy Spirit revival in the 70s and 80s, his Te Atatū Baptist Church was hundreds strong on a Sunday. Later though it shrunk, and there was a church split in which the younger support pastors to my father, who was by now the older, senior pastor, left with most of the youthful followers and formed their own thing. Dad stayed on, but my recollection by then was of a man burnt out, just as happens in other endeavours. A man who had to stay on for the stipend, as by then he was about to turn sixty, a Baptist minister nearly all his working life and with nothing else to do until retirement.

My presumption is, bluntly, that he was trapped. He couldn't change careers and, for example, go back to auditing, even though ostensibly he was still qualified. He was from the world of paper entries in a changing commercial world. There were not a lot of calls for ageing fire-and-brimstone preachers out in the 'real world'. Moreover, having lived in manses all our family life, Mum and Dad had made the mistake of never getting on the property ladder. This meant that despite being very disciplined with money (Mum more so than Dad), their savings were going backwards in comparison with house prices. Today of course it is even worse – exponentially so – but even in the late 90s it meant that when Mum and Dad finally bought, the house was not much.

My brothers and sisters see different versions of our parents, depending on their placement in our family and their age. I am the youngest of the six, and I am sure my siblings know a different father. Perhaps a more active, more fiery for good and bad father. More hands on, but also angrier. That wasn't my experience. I experienced an ageing man in his own world. He didn't hit me, but he didn't hug me. He was there, but he wasn't. We just got on without him, albeit his values for service and success were imbued in us hard. We, by his repetition around the dinner table and to the TV news, learned his hot takes and sayings. I feel some of my siblings may resent him, but I don't. A father who is distant though present isn't bad. While that's hardly a ringing endorsement, he was a faithful man who always provided, and he was a role model in his dedication to his church and serving the community.

It's not surprising that Dad was the way he was. As one of Natalie's favourite poets Philip Larkin wrote, 'They fuck you up, your mum and dad. They may not mean to, but they do.'

In fact, Dad was a reaction to and significant improvement on his upbringing; he was a much better dad than his dad. Alf, his father, was a hard man who drank, smoked and gambled money on racing that should have gone to his wife and children. I may be being unfair, but my sense is that he treated his wife, Naku, as a servant rather than a partner. Seeing this example, or lack of one, Dad's older sister Lorna never married or had partners, and went to San Francisco where she did very well. On her passing from cancer with no partner or children, my father inherited significantly and suddenly in later years he and Mum have been much more comfortable.

Dad also reacted to his childhood. Whereas his dad lived hard, my dad has never smoked, never touched a drop of liquor and went into the Christian ministry. Fanta, hamburgers and the like are as naughty as it gets. How he adores hamburgers, especially McDonald's. And he aspired for more for us kids. He was the opposite to his father. But there is something in the aphorism 'Give me a child until they are seven and I'll show you the man', and Dad was emotionally crippled. Aspirational, humorous, a good conversationalist with adults, a leader; but he was not one to touch or get deep and meaningful with. If that sounds contradictory for a man of God – well, it was.

The humour was brilliant when it was there. For all the emotional distance, he was a funny man. I could write a book of all his sayings. Among those I remember, he would often say he was on a seafood diet – see food and eat it – a Prince Tui Teka joke originally, I think. And it's true he has always had a childlike relationship to food. On the pulpit and at home he could be very talented, in a Billy T sort of a way. Joking and storytelling.

For himself, he was overwhelmingly very self-effacing and humble. He would talk himself down and say how lucky he was to have Mum. Perhaps it was a consciousness of the Māori in him, but deep down I don't believe he had a large or even healthy self-esteem. One of his well-known sayings for the family was: when in doubt, act dumb. Yet for us, his ambition was endless. He was relentless in his stated aim that all us kids should attain degrees, which he thought would provide endless opportunities. I said in my maiden speech in parliament that Naku Bridges wanted her children and grandchildren to have letters behind their names without really understanding what that meant. Well, Dad knew. It meant Opportunity in capital letters. For me, he was clear: I must do law. He would often say that he had never met a poor lawyer. He would also say that being rich isn't everything; but he'd rather be rich and unhappy than poor and unhappy. While not as significant in number as his Christian books, he had a healthy collection of financial self-help books of the 'I made millions from property and so can you' variety. These weren't for himself but were more about his dreams for us.

We all take traits from our parents, and from my dad I take a love of learning and thinking, and a desire for success. I now have a study in my garage with my books and things. Like he did, I retreat to it for peace and application. I've also adopted a similar approach to work as something more than a paycheque. It's a serious vocation.

But like my dad is a reaction to his father, I am also a reaction to him. I am a more loving husband to my partner, Natalie, and father to our three children, Emlyn, nine, Harry, seven, and Jemima, three. I learnt to ride a bike when I was ten and I taught myself; whereas all my kids rode early and we ride together all the time. Likewise for kisses and cuddles. If anything, we act more like an Italian family than a Kiwi one, with demonstrable displays of affection and kisses between the males in the household being commonplace.

My children are so precious, so worth it. Our eldest, Emlyn, has had to struggle through adversity. When he was born it was clear there was something unusual with his feet. They were both totally turned in. The doctors didn't say much at first, but the next day they confirmed he had had club feet. Over a few years he endured painful procedures and an operation, and wore a brace to keep his feet turned out most hours of the day at pre-school. As a result now he is a keen sportsman, playing hockey, rock climbing, tennis and more each week. His mother and the hospital staff deserve medals. Today he is a tough, durable boy but with a sweet, loving spirit. He loves animals and farms, so wants to be a vet or farmer. Never exactly top of my careers lists!

Harry, as our middle child, feels squeezed between his older sibling and his cute baby sister. But with his boyish good looks, charm, humour and fashion sense, the girls – some of them older – already love him. While he likes the idea of opening a restaurant, with his litigious character and chatter-box ways, I can see him taking on law like his daddy.

As for Jemima, with two older brothers, she can handle herself. At three years old she is both a characterful tomboy and a caring mummy to all her dollies. She's so savvy she could do anything.

However, because of how I've lived and worked 24/7 these last few years, I have catching up to do with all three kids and I am busy doing that. They change every week, and what I've now said about them here may be wrong in a fortnight. Natalie and I were together for over seven years before Emlyn came along. We never got around to children before that time because we were both busy professionally and enjoying our childless life together. I soon found that children rip the smug self-contentedness out of you, but even then I was buried in my work and was hardly Father of the Year.

Literally a month after Emlyn was born, John Key made me a minister outside Cabinet as Minister for Consumer Affairs, Associate Minister for Transport and Associate

Minister for Climate Change Issues. And while this was a privilege, I wasn't content with it. I needed to impress; I needed to become a Cabinet minister as quickly as possible. I didn't go to Wellington for the weather. So in Key's meritocratic executive, I set about working my backside off. I had done that in law and was always going to in politics as well. I thrust myself into the media with all manner of stunts and PR gimmicks. In Consumer Affairs, I recall banning magnets that could get stuck together in a stomach and kill children. I recall launching a war on wheel-clamping with some success. In Transport I was in charge of safety, and this got me on TV a lot for a low-level Minister. The consensus was that I'd had a great year professionally in 2012. In January 2013 I became a fully-fledged Cabinet minister: Minister of Labour and Minister of Energy and Resources. Over the rest of the Key–English government my rise continued, so that by the end I was number five in government and in the so-called 'kitchen-cabinet' that in reality ruled the land. This had all happened through sheer hard work and determination. Politics had received nearly all my time and energy, as I was away in the week and working in my home office most of the weekend, coming out to eat and sleep and maybe take a family walk or trip to the local playground if the kids were lucky.

The pressure to perform didn't let up when we moved in 2017 to Opposition benches. I knew Bill English wouldn't stay. That was inevitable, and I was clear in my own mind that I was the best person to lead National and the Opposition. As Opposition Leader, if anything I worked even harder than I had as a senior government minister. As a minister you have the comfort of your discrete policy priorities and of knowing that someone else is ultimately the boss. As leader, when all is said and done, there is no one else. I was very fortunate to have brilliant counsel and friendship from Paula Bennett and others, but in the end I felt personal pressure to perform to keep our party poll numbers high. In hindsight, I probably focused on these weekly numbers too much at the expense of the bigger picture. But I always lived knowing that, were there a bad TV poll, the small camps in caucus around Todd Muller and Judith Collins would become larger.

When your number is up, it is up. While I managed to claw us back to pole position following the Christchurch terror attack and then the Whakaari/White Island eruptions, where there had been natural rallying effects for Jacinda Ardern, Covid-19 proved too much. We can all (over)analyse what could have been done differently. And I don't think there is any doubt that continuity of my leadership would have resulted in a better election result for National. Nevertheless, Covid-19 and TVNZ's twice-daily briefings were insurmountable challenges for any leader of the Opposition in an election year.

On the day I lost the leadership of the National Party, I felt those around me were sadder for me than I was. While I had given it all I had and was disappointed, I was fine. I meant what I said at my press conference, conceding to Todd Muller; I'd told Natalie that morning that if I won then I won, but if I lost, we won. I made a solemn resolution to myself upon losing the leadership that Natalie and the kids would receive the benefit of my career change. I would learn from my dad by being more than simply a physical presence with my mind somewhere else. I would be more present as a hands-on, loving father, much more involved in their lives from now on.

To date, that has proved to be the case. While I am still no picture of perfection, the boys and I have had many firsts lately, from tramping escapades and fishing trips to movie nights and card games. As for Jemima, she is the apple of Daddy's eye, and I need to learn how to say no to her, so tightly am I wrapped around her little finger. As well there are the important, mundane routines that I am embarrassed to say I didn't do before. The youngest now get their milk bottles made by me, their bedtime stories read by me, and I share picking them up from school when I am not at parliament.

Yes, everything comes at a cost. Today we live in a time of work–life balance. The harsh reality, however, is that I chose to give politics my all from 2008 to 2020. While there may be some genius out there who can be both a perfect spouse *and* a senior politician, I am not one of them. Key family milestones were skirted over. While I was at the births of all my children, I was generally gone within twenty-four hours. Birthdays, prizegivings and the like, I've either been present and watching the clock, or away.

In 2019, for example, my boys had a shared birthday party on 16 March. Family, school friends and parents were all coming to our Tauranga home. The night before, however, was the evening of the Christchurch terror attack. Prime Minister Ardern called me to ask if, as leader of the Opposition, I could attend visits in Christchurch in the aftermath of the atrocities. I hustled it to Wellington to be on board the Air Force jet the next morning. I of course had to attend and make nothing light of those major events. But for my little children, they simply see that Daddy hasn't prioritised their special moments. Time after time. I could tell dozens of stories of big family moments lost or not made the most of because I put government and politics as a priority, whereas if I had made commitments to my family I would oftentimes let them down at the last second. Nothing is for free. I was always on the clock. Family came second.

I am not out of time though. As I've said, I am in catch-up mode. What I've learned in the last few months is that, while it's not easy and it takes adjustment, you can catch up. Unlike my father was with me, I've always been huggy and kissy with my children. In that regard, things stay the same. But now my kids get my most precious gift: the gift of my time.

Resilience is an overused word today, but not when it comes to children. They are wondrously, fabulously, resilient. Where a year ago they all knew I couldn't be at their events or make them those toasted sandwiches, now they know that I can, and so now they expect it like I've been doing it forever. They've noticed the change and adapted to it with relish.

My son Emlyn sang Elton John's 'Crocodile Rock' at his school prizegiving at the end of last year. I helped him prepare with a lot of practice, encouragement and all the advice a forty-four-year-old politician could give on how to sing Elton John the best. Not only did Emlyn make it through the show (which is more than Elton did, when I forked out for us to see him perform at Mount Smart), but he knocked it out of the park. Other parents came up and said how amazing he was. Maybe they were just being nice, but I reckon they meant it. And Emlyn was delighted. That's every bit as satisfying as politics.

I am not a natural-born father. In many ways, law and politics come more easily to me as an adult than parenting. My default is to be reading an intellectual text or discussing the new US–China Cold War with like-minded people. To switch from that to child's-talk is far from child's play. But perfection isn't possible in either politics or parenting. As I lean in to my responsibility as a dad to Emlyn, Harry and Jemima, each with their very different characteristics and quirks, I learn and grow, and we get there.

7
INTROVERSION

I ONCE LEARNED A GOOD WORKING DEFINITION FOR extroversion and introversion. If people energise you, you're an extrovert. If they de-energise you, you're an introvert. Carl Jung saw extroverts as drawn to the external life of activities and people, whereas introverts tend to their inner worlds of thought and feeling. I believe personality shapes us perhaps just as much as our gender or ethnicity. According to Jung, the single-most important determinant of personality is where we fall on the introvert–extrovert spectrum. I think I agree with him.

I'm a high-functioning introvert. That doesn't mean I don't like people. I love company, for a time. In fact, one of my favourite things in the universe is an intimate dinner with several people – talking, sharing good conversation and food. As my waistline attests, I attend a lot of functions and dinners, and I have a great time. But eventually I want them to stop so I can recharge in my own thoughts and world.

Yes, there are introverts who cower if a person comes to the door. Shyness is a first cousin of introversion. But on the other side, many of the world's best performers have been introverts. I remember being incredibly sad as a lad when Freddie Mercury died in the late 80s. I remember on TV the flowers piled up outside his London home and that it had been something called HIV, which I hadn't heard of before. He was the greatest showman of the twentieth century, and I believe he was an introvert.

I asked Natalie how I could describe my introversion. She says it's very easy. She says my idea of heaven is being alone in a comfy lounge chair in a closed room that's in a house full of my family going about their activities. All my family would be around, but not with me. There's some truth in this. In my own world, thinking my own thoughts. No noise. I like people close but distant, if you get what I mean.

This hasn't always been easy for Natalie, nor has her extroversion been perfect for me. To stay fully charged, she needs people. I need study or Netflix time. As I mentioned in the marriage chapter, we used to have a lot of misunderstandings about this, with her seeing my quiet time as a rejection of her, and my seeing her demand for people and energy as a rejection of me. After a long week at parliament, arguing for what I believe in and interacting with type-A person after type-A person, I come back to Tauranga to the refuge of home. Often Natalie will want to go out or have a party at ours. I want to curl up, with her next to me, reading a le Carré or a long history book. Fortunately Natalie is an easygoing extrovert, and over time we've met in the middle. Often we will go out, but sometimes we won't. Date nights are now relatively regular and meet both our needs: quality time talking, but not too much.

Closing time on a social outing or party at ours has often been an issue. Many a party has involved me dragging Natalie from the venue or just putting myself to bed (sometimes to secretly read) while the dancing continued below. I've got better at not being too weird and at staying sociable, and more often than not Natalie and I negotiate leaving times that meet her needs and mine. We've come a long way since the early years. A bit like using medicine to regulate a problem, we can discuss, negotiate and regulate.

I remember some of the bad times from the past, however, which demonstrate a fair bit about how I tick. Bruce is my schoolmate and was my best man at our wedding, as I was at his. At his wedding in the earlier years of mine and Natalie's marriage, he also coincidentally married a beautiful Polish woman, Marianna. We were in some small city, I forget which, up near the Ukraine border. Polish wedding celebrations last twelve hours or more, from late afternoon, overnight and into the next day. I started the party with a hiss and a roar. I enjoy performing for a crowd, and I took my best man role to gee up the crowd seriously. I led the drinking (there was a bottle of vodka for each guest), the dancing, the eating, the speechifying. But, and you can see where this is going, early on (Natalie would say *very* early on) I got peopled out. Yes, some of it was the vodka, but it was also my introvert batteries running low. Come a certain time, I had to leave and I made Natalie leave also. She has never let me live that misstep down. There was so much party left, but I was not geared up for Eastern European weddings.

In a brilliant book called *Quiet: The Power of Introverts in a World That Can't Stop Talking,* Susan Cain says that in the Western world we have an 'Extrovert Ideal' which is 'the omnipresent belief that the ideal self is gregarious, alpha, and comfortable in the spotlight'.[8] Allied to this view is that leaders are extroverts. Nowhere is this view stronger than in politics, though of course law and other areas also cling to the myth. At its logical conclusion, this means we all need to be seen as extroverts. So many people, I believe, fake it even when it's obviously inauthentic. Perhaps I have faked it at times as well, but I wouldn't be surprised if you'd thought that as a politician I would just naturally be a big-time extrovert.

Great leaders and politicians aren't always extroverts. Some are, but many aren't. John Key clearly is an extrovert. He loves people and to talk. He thinks through talking, and I admire this about him. It's what works for him; it's authentically him. John also loves to be invited to events. I have seen him turn up to things and thought to myself, 'Why on earth are you here, JK?' But I know the answer. He loves being there with everyone. He is energised by them.

But I doubt that Helen Clark is an extrovert. I don't know Helen well, and while our politics and perspectives are different, I respect her and I see myself in her, if I can say that. Helen is serious and likes introverted ways best, I reckon. Bill English is a bit harder to say, and he could in fact straddle the two personality types, but in my opinion he is not a card-carrying member of the Extrovert Club. I recall many a conversation with Bill, and let's just say he's not a chatty one. Some of this is Southern man stuff, but it also must be the personality inside him. He doesn't mind silence, which gives him space to think.

As for Jacinda, while I feel I know her pretty well in a funny sort of way from our regular mornings back in the day as 'Young Guns' on *Breakfast* with Paul Henry, through to many dealings as MPs and while she has led New Zealand, I honestly couldn't say. Her brand is so strong that it's relatively hard to know who the real Jacinda is. Earlier leaders, like Helen and John, were in the public eye more spontaneously, so you got a sense for the real them through the good and bad. I am not sure what's exactly behind Jacinda the product – extrovert or introvert.

You might think that my father is an introvert from all I have said about him, his lack of family skills and his office garage. And yet just as this whole area is complex, so was my father. I actually think on balance he's an extrovert. His problems with family stem more from his own upbringing than his personality. When he was in his office it was to work, not massively out of a joy of solitude. While I haven't detailed this part of his personality, Heath was a real people-person. He was made for Pentecostalism because inside of him there was a natural-born salesman, an evangelist, and it was the Lord he was selling. I remember great embarrassment throughout my childhood as Dad would go up to complete strangers and strike up conversations. He'd be right in their body space, they'd smell his breath as he shot the breeze with them and maybe talked about sport and life.

The in-the-face thing is worth dwelling on. While he wouldn't touch people, he was, I recall, always weirdly close. Emotionally he didn't get it, had no sense of personal body space. And it's perhaps for this reason that Dad always had on his person the old Lions Mints you could buy from the local garage. He wouldn't go anywhere without these, his handkerchief and his small black comb. Search his blazers – he has always worn buttoned shirts and a suit jacket or blazer whether rain, hail or shine – and the mints would always be there. Quite smart, really, as they weren't a sugar-filled lolly that I as a kid would pester him for.

NATIONAL IDENTITY

We could be at the mall, the takeaways, the zoo. It really didn't matter. Up Dad would walk to someone and start talking. Sometimes this would result in rejection, but that was water off a duck's back. It was like dating for Dad: a few rejections for a kiss now and then was worth it. Many times he'd be engaged with the other people for half an hour. Like Key, the reason was simple. He loved it and enjoyed them. It was just what he did. The someone could be a guy or girl from any walk of life. I remember him bowling up and chatting with Sir Ed Hillary at the Copper Kettle café in Ngatea. I'm not entirely sure Ed and June wanted Dad to sit and join them, but he did. I also recall him introducing me to an old, frail David Lange at the Royal Easter Show in Auckland. Dad had voted Lange, but was disappointed by the Margaret Pope business.

I can do what Dad did and I don't mind it, sometimes even enjoy it. As a politician I have door-knocked thousands of doors, walked many a shopping mall and polished how to strike up a chat, maximising the chance of successful engagement rather than a rebuff. But if it was between that and a good book, well, you know what I'd choose.

My mum, Ruth Bridges? She is a wonderful introvert. She loves people, children especially, and now has twenty grandchildren. But yet she is an introvert. I know this because I know what she prefers. She prefers her solo-projects: jobs at home, being in her garden, reading her book, TV shows in the evening. Today Mum and Dad come and visit us, but those visits are very practical and almost business-like. There's no mucking around; when they are done they are done. Mum checks we're all okay, has her cup of tea, and after giving us the jam she's preserved or some free oranges from church this week, she is gone – she must finish painting the fence, planting her lettuces, or reading the new book she's got out from Mount Maunganui Library.

This is a real contrast to Natalie's family, who have such difficulty saying goodbye that to end the communing together is a potential personal slight. The point comes where they are there, physically or virtually on WhatsApp, and it's clearly time for everyone to move on. But this invariably involves several more stories and discussions before the final goodbye. Natalie's mum will say bye, then they will all talk some more. Then there will be another goodbye and some more talking. At the end there is a ritualistic goodbye where the words are said over and over again, 'Bye, bye, bye, bye, bye …' and on it goes slowly trailing off, until it somehow feels acceptable to stop the call or get into the car and drive away.

To be fair to my mum – a practical sort – she also knows how busy I am and when she visits she probably thinks I haven't got much time. These days, if Dad's visiting as well, she's thinking too that he can't be out for too long. If he's not, she's thinking he can't be left alone at home too long with his dementia and other ailments. And Mum deeply values her independence. She wants her own home where she can do these things I've mentioned just how she wants to, alone. She must have the kitchen as she wants it and a proper garden. Her home is her castle.

I know this because we fell out a number of years ago when I tried to encourage Mum into a retirement village that I thought would be perfect for her socialising and with the added support for Dad. But she doesn't want socialising. She wants her own space and her own garden. In this, Mum takes after her father, who lived alone for many years at Waihi Beach after he sold his Waihi farm, and was happiest in a sunny room listening to orchestras and operas. Indeed, this is how he died at eighty-seven, living alone as he had for many years after his wife passed on, having just come in from mowing the lawn and resting in his Lay-Z-Boy while the orchestra was at full volume.

I wonder if farmers, with their independent streak, tend towards introversion more often than not? Certainly I'd say they tend to use few words, and I am not sure it would be a great job for a massive extrovert. Cows don't speak English, last time I checked. But what I've noticed is that work ethic feeds into introversion. Like Mum's old man, or my granddad, my mum has a relentless work ethic. Bringing up six children over a period of nearly thirty years, she lived for us, and on her and Dad's income that meant industriousness. Sewing, knitting, planting, stewing, every day all year round. People-time can be an extravagance, I am sure my mum thinks, when there is work to do. And there is always work to do. Better to finish stewing all the rhubarb Alan dropped around than just sit with a few friends gassing. And once you think like this out of necessity, it's hard to shake that work ethic when all the kids are gone and you no longer need to stew all that bloody rhubarb, as good as it is on Weetbix or porridge. These qualities of introversion – work ethic, flintiness and independence – I take from my mum. I take them whether I want to or not.

My mother and I, we love each other deeply. Yet our relationship is so conflicted by latent disputes. She's shaped me more than anyone. I get my capital letter Values like 'ambition', 'religion' and 'service' from Dad, but all the consonants and vowels, the whole alphabet, really, comes from Mum. My intricacies and faults, my qualities and hang-ups. It's because she was there while he was distant. She loved, served, comforted and cradled me, and in so doing, imbued me with her ways.

In recent times, I've realised my difficulty to enjoy and to laze around comes from her. Mum is from the generation that can't enjoy a meal out because 'I could make this at home for a third of the price' and 'This is not a proper meal – $28 for a couple of mouthfuls!' I tell her to lighten up and enjoy, but it's no use. We fall out. And I sometimes have resented her latently, passively, quietly but aggressively. We have also fallen out at times over her worries about my political career. While Dad has simply gone along for the ride, enjoying and being proud to have a son who is a Member of Parliament, Mum takes all criticism to heart, poring over online abuse and getting concerned by media about me. Then she tells me about it, making me feel worse about garbage that would otherwise not have affected me. I worry because she worries; for me, her distress is worse to handle than the original issue. Asking her not to read any of it is like asking the swallow not to fly south in winter. To make matters worse, we haven't been able to resolve these conflicts, whether latent or above the surface. We haven't had a language or a shared style to resolve these things, or maybe like some feuding hillbillies, we haven't wanted the dispute to end.

So it's all been left unsaid. Perhaps our shared introversion is part of the problem, for at least in a barney with Natalie we always have it out and conclude the matter. As an extrovert, she's not one *not* to talk about it. Natalie calls the spade a $%#@&# shovel and we get on with it. But recently I've made clear to Mum that, when I visit with the children or she comes round, I want a mum and a grandma, not a worried political pundit. It took a bit to pluck up the gumption and have the hard talk, but we did. I am not sure Mum quite understands where I am coming from, but to her remarkable credit there isn't politics in our relationship anymore, just everything else. And that's something amazing about my mum. There is never malice or looking back with her. Her applied Christianity means forgive and forget, and her farm girl practicality means we get on with it.

All in all, I am a high-functioning introvert. I've learned to not be a complete weirdo and to meet in the middle with my extrovert wife, but I wouldn't change my personality for a minute. It's no disability but a God-given privilege. That moment of solitude, when early in the morning before everyone else is up I hear the birds in my garden, is life-affirming and strengthening to me. When I read something late at night while my household sleeps happily around me, sometimes it's so beautiful I cry. And I haven't given up all weirdnesses. When I was younger and studying, or just reading in my room, I became obsessed about silence. I would wear earplugs and then sometimes my dad's lawn-mowing earmuffs over top in order to cut out every voice, every car and every cricket. What bliss.

I'm not quite as bad today, but I do work hard to ensure my kids watch cartoons a long way away from me if I can. I often turn down Natalie's constant talkback radio, and I am forever lowering the volume when the kids play ZM or other nonsense on Alexa. The sound of silence, or as close as I can get to it without mutiny from my kids and wife, is still a beautiful thing to me.

Workwise, I have been lucky to always be in professions and high enough up food chains to have my own office with walls and a door that I can shut! When I started in law, I had my own office with a view over Auckland Harbour and I have never looked back. The idea of open plan doesn't thrill me. As a Cabinet minister, then Leader of the Opposition, and still now as a senior MP, I've always been blessed with big offices to call my own. One thing that's been important to me is that when I am alone, I like my door shut. It's about noise but also privacy and work, a sense no one is watching me and I am in my own safe space to do my best. Staff have always thought this strange, particularly in this modern world of constant chat and collaborative workplaces. But in the end, when I am trying to focus, weird or not, I find colleagues chatting about the movie they watched last night makes me stressed. I can eliminate it, so I do.

I should say though that, as far as I know, I have always been a popular boss. I'm no Christmas Grinch. Not all MPs and ministers can say this, but I have been blessed with incredibly loyal staff with whom I have been deeply grateful to work and learn from. I believe the feeling has always been mutual.

In the end, there is much literature to make clear that independent work in solitude is often superior for creativity and excellence. The modern groupthink in our business world and social sector, which makes teamwork its own religion, is misguided. I'm not saying that 'brainstorming' and 'white-boarding', et cetera, don't add value. In the right time and place, coming together is essential after necessary independent thinking by colleagues. But if done all the time, it strikes me as less fruitful generally and certainly for us introverts specifically. We need our creative space to do great things. If you don't believe me just ask Einstein, JK Rowling, Steve Jobs, Mahatma Ghandi, Marie Curie, Bill Gates, Warren Buffett, Meryl Streep or Barack Obama. I can't compare myself to any of these geniuses, but we share one common trait: we are all introverts who believe in working alone for the best results.

God told King Solomon that He would grant to him one wish, any wish, and Solomon asked for wisdom. Because he hadn't asked for a Lamborghini and some quality time with Cindy Crawford (I am showing my age), God not only granted the wish but gave him a double-portion, making him the wisest person who ever lived. There is no doubt Solomon chose well in his request (and to be fair, he already had a shed-load of gold and more wives and concubines than any other biblical character). In Proverbs it says, 'Wisdom is the principal thing; therefore get wisdom. And in all your getting, get understanding.'

Knowing yourself is a key component of being wise. You can know your times-tables and even your quantum physics, but if you don't understand yourself, that's not much good. Wisdom and self-perception are more important than all the knowledge of Stephen Hawking. I hope that in my thinking about my personality and introversion, you have also been provoked into thinking about your personality. Like Proverbs says, get understanding. It's worth more than its weight in gold.

8
POLITICS

POLITICS IN NEW ZEALAND HAS BECOME A BIT OF A YOUNG person's sport. Our current prime minister is younger than I am, and I am only in my mid-forties. Regrettably, there seems to be a feeling that if you're in your sixties, you're probably ready for pasture.

In this regard we are an outlier. I won't labour the point, but by way of contrast take the United States. There they run a gerontocracy; in recent times you seem to need to be in your seventies to run for president, and it's common to see senators in their eighties, heck even their nineties. I'd like to think a happy medium is desirable – a House of Representatives should be just that – some young, some middle-aged, some more, *ahem*, senior, just like the wider population.

I took an interest in public life young. We weren't a political household, but when we ate dinner round the big table after watching the six o'clock news, we would talk about it. I recall conversations about Muldoon and Lange, and that my older brother Tim fancied himself as a libertarian. Get the government out of our lives, he would preach! He was backing Bob Jones's New Zealand Party in the early 80s.

In addition to discussions about the issues of the day, our home was a good breeding ground for politics in as much as we mixed with a lot of people. As a church house, people from all walks of life were wandering through – those a bit better off from West Harbour and those down and out, in need of a meal. We saw it all and became comfortable with it all.

A seminal moment for me was in my reading. Aunty Lorna, my dad's only sibling, had given us little biographical picture books of every US President. At age eleven I bought a book with my pocket money that my son Emlyn now has, called the Usborne *Introduction to Politics and Governments: A beginner's guide to political words and ideas*. As an Usborne book it was quasi-comic-like, filled with pictures and diagrams and fact boxes, and it told me the story of politics from nationalism and patriotism to liberalism and conservatism (woke-ism was not yet invented). I learned my communism from my socialism, fascism from democracy, as well as about elections, voting systems and the separation of powers. What's more, I loved it. I'd caught a fire that would never leave. Politics was fascinating and, who knows, maybe it could even be for me.

As a political tragic, I then began as a pre-teen, then a young teen, watching more news, following things, looking at newspapers and listening to that taboo for the chattering classes, talkback radio. It all seemed amazing, so vital and significant. A bit like my first sip of instant coffee, also around this time, suddenly I saw life in full colour and I was hooked. I even recall calling talkback – sadly can't remember what about, but I am sure it was incredibly important. In any event, reading and radio introduced me to the popular, and populist, discussions of the day. I was becoming, albeit in an armchair sort of a way, a politico.

Then in 1992 in Te Atatū North, outside my Foodtown, I took my first fateful and practical step. I saw some National Party people putting up a sign for a public meeting or something. It was my moment. As a sixteen-year-old I bowled on over and asked if I could join. I could and I did, and now I have been a member of the New Zealand National Party close to thirty years and counting.

Now Te Atatū wasn't the most dynamic electorate for the National Party in our country. But it did have good people with good hearts. In 1993 a gent called Tracy Adams was our candidate and he was up against a teacher at my school, Labour candidate then MP and minister, Chris Carter. I sometimes spare a thought for the Tracys of the world – they would make reasonable enough MPs. And yet for them it just doesn't happen. For some like me, through luck or whatever, it just does.

With much zeal I did everything and more that Tracy wanted: delivering pamphlets, helping with signs, attending meetings and committees. At one level it was a complete waste of time. Probably I'd have been better off doing homework and chasing girls. But what it did do was by osmosis teach me grassroots politics and the values and culture of the National Party, the biggest beast in New Zealand politics.

Every political party has a particular culture, rules both spoken and unspoken. Some of these things are obvious, but some take years to pick up at the monthly meetings and the regional and national conferences. Some of them are tropes, things to say that will get a row of nodding grey heads: like 'farming and small business are the backbone of our economy', or 'tough on crime' and 'welfare cheats'. Received truths not to be messed with. Others are religious aversions to tax, to unions and to the Labour Party! Some go even deeper as to what people expect you to look and sound like. The National Party rank and file are about big, strong hands and handshakes. Look them in the eye, son, and tell it like it is. Straight talk it, son.

I've no doubt, by the way, that the New Zealand Labour Party has its own peculiar ways, probably rather more of a darned wool and colourful cardigans culture than firm handshakes. But my tribe was National, and over the next few years I attended everything I could and through trial and error learned it better than almost anyone from grassroots to the top table.

For myself in Te Atatū I also set about trying to achieve some personal political goals: leadership within the Auckland (or Northern, as it was known) Young Nationals. To achieve this I needed to set up a Young Nationals branch, which I quickly learned required twenty members. If I didn't do this, the Young Nats hierarchy, which met every month at the CBD offices on Vincent Street, wouldn't let me attend. After all, I was from Te Atatū, not Remuera or the Shore, and sixteen to their early twenties.

Not put off, I duly begged, borrowed and stole to get my twenty. A brother, his friends, my mates, knowingly or not became members for a couple of bucks. They were mostly okay with it as long as I paid the fee. Saying it like this today sounds, well, a lot like Aussie-style branch-stacking or something. But heck, I was sixteen and I wanted to be part of the Northern Young Nats Executive. Needs, my friend, must.

Eventually I got there, held an AGM, took the minutes and was elected Te Atatū Young Nats Chair, probably the first and last ever. I then started attending the Vincent Street Young Nats meetings with the Carrick Grahams (son of Doug), the Slaters, Shane Frith and other lesser lights. I also started attending the more senior meetings, becoming friends with many still active today, such as John Slater, Alistair Bell and Peter Goodfellow.

I became friendly with MPs – such a thrill at the time. Wayne Mapp, who'd buy me a beer. Good old Mappy. Clem Simich, very dapper with his pocket handkerchief. And my local West Auckland MP, who I ended up doing a lot for, Brian Neeson. Poor old Brian, while a good local battler, had the great misfortune of being promoted through electorate boundary changes to eventually hold the safe seat of Helensville. Too safe. This made it ripe for the picking by a guy who looked like an MP for a safe seat; who, unlike Brian, was a Kiwi trader recently back in New Zealand: John Key. Contrary to what Wikipedia says, I never voted in the Key–Neeson selection battle, as by then I was in Tauranga trying to lock up crims. Key won by a nose. The rest, like they say, is history.

Over time I became Northern Young Nats Chair, but the race for power didn't stop there. Back in the 90s, the governing body of the National Party comprised of regional representatives, the President, and a bunch of Vice Presidents representing various groups such as Māori and women. There was another VP for Young Nats, elected each year at the Young Nats AGM, held alongside the senior National Conference. With stars in my eyes, and in fairness as Chair of the biggest region that gave me a chance, I began seeking cross-regional support before the big conference in 1997 in Christchurch. My competitor was a Cantabrian, Tim Hurdle, working for a new MP by the name of Gerry Brownlee. Tim went on to work in the Beehive during my time as a minister, and for Todd Muller and briefly Judith Collins as Opposition leaders.

Well, I brought a knife to a gunfight and learned a few lessons over that campaign about what not to do. The main lesson was probably around not pissing off a serving Prime Minister, the Rt Hon Jim Bolger, very shortly before he was rolled by Jenny Shipley. I will get to that.

My campaign began months in advance. I developed a brochure and had to make toll calls round the country, all a big expense for a twenty-year-old kid working at Foodtown. I borrowed Mum's little Toyota Starlet – it was like an unsafe sewing machine with a body and wheels – and legged it down to meetings in Hamilton and Palmerston North trying to round up votes.

Then we got close to the conference, which turned out to be the beginning of the end of Bolger. This was mostly because Jenny was on manoeuvres, but with a walk-in role played by yours truly. You see, Young Nats had a little newsletter, and as Chair I ostensibly had oversight of this fine periodical called *Club Nat*. The reality was, I naively left it to others, and on the eve of the conference one of them wrote a column excoriating poor old Jim as an 'Aunt Daisy' who was allowing the kids – Winston and co – to run amok, and whose time as leader was up.

Well, on the first morning of the conference, as this newsletter was making waves, Jim wasn't happy. His enemies were clearly using it to play him. He then did a couple of things which, albeit overreactions, I suppose were understandable given the late phase of his leadership. The conference really was the beginning of his end.

The conference was at the now-demolished Hotel Grand Chancellor in Christchurch. Having already put hundreds of dollars into the conference with brochures, calls and petrol, I was staying at a backpackers' a block or two away. I showered in the communal showers and then suited up in my one good suit to look as if I had just come from my hotel suite.

Peter Kiely, now a great friend and ever a legal fix-it man for the party, had summoned me to a meeting with the PM at lunchtime of the first full day of proceedings. I was ushered by Kiely into a small room taken up by a large table full of older men. There was the PM, his chief of staff, the President, and other seniors such as John Slater – as an Aucklander, my only ally. Jim felt I had defamed him, and Peter Kiely and Geoff Thompson gave a rundown on defamation law for good effect, notwithstanding that much of what they were saying was questionable. Jim then yelled quite a bit. My recollection is he called me a bastard. I was expected to apologise and agree to say nothing to the media. I agreed. Jim was clearly worried this would undermine his conference and leadership, already looking rocky. I then remember specifically a young female staff member brought Jim a plate of sushi, very exotic in 1996. He ate it while the rest of us watched him.

The next day was the Young Nats AGM. And it was around this time that Jim made his second play. My campaigning was all pissing in the wind, because after our Saturday sushi meet-and-greet Jim not so subtly told the youth delegates they should be voting Hurdle. As a result, my chances of being Youth Vice President and thus on the Board of the National Party were dashed on the rocks, although, to be fair, Tim Hurdle had the home crowd advantage and was a much more experienced operator than I was then. To Tim's credit he made me his deputy; even while losing I was climbing the greasy pole.

I left the conference worried and dejected. On the Monday I received my first ever mention in the *New Zealand Herald*. Bernard Orsman had caught a sniff of the story: 'Newsletter lands young delegate in the bad books'. I was reported as a 'no comment', my first of many to journos over the years. Bernard said I was 'shaken after being given legal advice and a stern dressing down', and he made clear Bolger had undermined my Presidency bid. Unnamed sources said, 'the hierarchy's actions were over the top and destroyed the notion of free speech in the party'.

As a slow learner, it wasn't the end of my controversies with print. Just four months later I oversaw the production of another newsletter which the *Herald* enjoyed. Again,

Bernard was the writer: 'Young Nats liken Peters to Saddam', a comparison on the basis that both individuals were 'an unfathomable threat to stability that is best removed from power'. In what must be my first public sledge of Winston and he back at me, he said that the analogy was ridiculous and showed a great deal of immaturity.

Not to be deterred, having lived to fight another day, I decided to try again for Youth Vice President in 1999, this time under the reign of Jenny. And this time the rules had changed largely because of what I put poor Bolger through. To ensure a more managed democracy, where the powers that be got who they wanted, the vote moved from just Young Nats to the floor of the main conference – several hundred senior delegates on top of the smattering of young people. Oldies now chose the Young Nats leader. Thus, to win, a bigger effort was involved. I sent out letters and brochures and paid for other paraphernalia. I even had a fancy badge I was giving away, 'Simon for Vice Pres', and T-shirts. It had cost me a fortune that I didn't really have from my Foodtown and Auckland Club jobs, but I knew that to win, I had to be professional.

The weekend came in Wellington at the Town Hall. It was election year, and election conferences are always in the capital. My speech was a cracker – written by an ally, Scott Simpson, now MP for Coromandel – and with a PowerPoint presentation done by David Farrar, something that was at the time very modern. I delivered the speech well, and soon-to-be MPs Simon Power and Chester Borrows said they'd voted for me off the back of it. Bill Birch told me it was the speech of the conference. Sadly though I still lost, this time by a more respectable margin to Dan Gordon, who like Tim was also from Canterbury. Dan had outgunned and outspent me. Today, Dan is Mayor of the Waimakariri District.

Still, I learned a lot: what not to do, and how to count, about the regions and how they played things, sometimes against Auckland, and how to hold myself. Yes, I had wasted huge quantities of time and money I didn't really have, but I was being trained for the future – so that winning Tauranga and even the leadership of the National Party were less difficult, more understandable propositions thanks to my efforts with the Young Nats.

Soon after the conference I left Young Nats, but the Auckland Party made me a deputy regional chair and an electorate chair of that safe National seat of Mount Roskill (a long-time Labour stronghold, then held by Phil Goff). I ran the election campaign that year for our candidate, Avondale College principal Phil Raffills, who was tragically dying of cancer. The next year I started as a lawyer and soon enough I became further enmeshed in the establishment in the party, on the rules committee chaired by Peter Kiely and the list-ranking committee, which ranks MPs and candidates for the election.

As I look back, a couple of things strike me about my experiences as a young activist. First, if we look at Young Nats in the 2020s, they seem very precious in comparison to what I experienced. While I was bullied by a serving prime minister, for them, the slightest criticism can trigger a complaint. Today, I sometimes wonder if they have more in common politically and culturally with Young Greens and Labour Youth than with the National Party I grew up with.

In my day, on our side of the political fence you were either a conservative or a libertarian, two long-standing proud traditions. We didn't whine about identity politics. We had robust, principled debates on prostitution law reform, tax policy, voluntary student unionism and the like. Think young John Banks versus young Lindsay Perigo. That was the Young Nats in the 90s; not all in groupthink agreement that identity politics is all that matters, as today's lot sometimes are. That said, I do acknowledge one thing about today's youth activists and myself. We both cared enough to join up, to add our name and voice to the cause as members. To many that probably doesn't sound like much, but by God it is.

Once upon a time, certainly in the days of Piggy Muldoon, National had many hundreds of thousands of members. Going back even further, Young Nationals was so large – in the several tens of thousands – that many attended to find a wife or a husband. I still meet people today who tell me they met their Betsy at a Young Nationals dance in Paeroa. Good times indeed. By my era, the Young Nats would have been lucky to have a thousand or so in a good year. Today, the organisation is very niche. I suspect the other political parties' youth movements are much the same, if not weaker. And it's not just the youth. The total membership of National, as with all political parties, has shrunk and shrunk.

As you sit here reading this, you may feel this doesn't matter. But it really does. Without vibrant memberships, there are not enough people to help at elections – the signs, the pamphlets – but, more than that, there aren't the people to bring forward ideas and policies. This way, parties become susceptible to capture by fringe groups with a barrow to push.

If all that is needed for evil to triumph is for good people to do nothing, we must be closer than we've been. I've written this book because we are in a cultural fog. And it's a fog of complacency among the overwhelming majority of Kiwis. Boat, bach, Beamer – or even just a boat, and many couldn't give a monkey's. A foreign enemy could be invading and some would say we should stop being hysterical. As long as we can still go for a fish, she'll be right. But she won't be right. Over time, our institutions and national life are eroding, as people won't join up and join in.

Let's understand: this isn't simply a party political phenomenon. Recently I chatted to a couple of older women about the organisations they're involved in. They hearkened back, not sorrowfully but perhaps wistfully, to when they first joined up in the 60s. In those days nearly everyone did, whether for Zonta, Rural Women, the JCs, Rotary, Lions, the Golf Club, the Coastguard or the Football Association. Today, next to no one does unless there is something tangible in it for them – for example, a specific networking opportunity where they might personally benefit. One woman I was talking to also made the shrewd observation that younger generations, millennials in particular, will only come onboard if it's very short term and a discrete cause. Think Black Lives Matter or #MeToo. I don't entirely knock this. Both these causes make serious and important points. But there is much more to a strong, healthy, democratic society than the odd cause. For strong institutions and a flourishing country from your suburb all the way to the Beehive, we need more people to turn up day in and day out, whether it's convenient and fits with your Pilates appointment or not.

Let's accept that there are some good excuses not to turn up. Society has changed a lot – like, a whole lot. Both partners work full time. Dinner isn't on the table at 5.45 pm sharp. As we work in the rat race to pay the mortgage and 'voluntary' school fees, we are kept busy. By the time we've watched a little of *The Bachelor* or Netflix, surfed the net for porn or penguins, it's time for bed. Unless you're a zealot for a cause, there is little time for giving back, save for a few likes to a good cause on Facebook or Instagram. Somehow, though, these good excuses – work, Pilates, Netflix, fishing, take your pick – aren't quite good enough. Deeper civic involvement can't just be for other people. Because increasingly there aren't those other people around.

Allied to this cultural malaise is a worry I have about how people become MPs these days. I came up as a political junkie in the volunteer part of the National Party. But I also had what my dad would call my tent ministry. Around 50 AD, St Paul's vocation was to convert people to Christianity – but his day job, which he needed to pay the bills and for street cred, was making tents. For me, I was a lawyer. I got the degrees, I practised for several years, and when I came to parliament there was a meaningful sense that I was giving up a serious career for Tauranga and our country. I came to parliament with some outside skills. The same is true for many others. My mate Mark Mitchell, MP for Whangaparaoa, was a senior policeman and brought that acumen and experience. Others have farmed, developed, taught and led. In Labour of old there were tradespeople, organisers, people from all walks of life. And for a House of Representatives, this is how it should be.

Yet today we have the rise of the Beehive politician. From university straight to the Beehive, where they work for an MP or a minister before they stand for a seat or the list. If we are lucky, they may have some comms or lobbying experience for a big corporate that probably had a monopoly in its field.

Experience in small or medium enterprises, the backbone of this land, fighting for survival, competing on a not-so-level playing field? Not so much.

This is a worry for a bunch of reasons, but one straight off the bat is a lack of experience. They don't have it from real communities in the way we expect of and deserve from our representatives. Everything for them has been politics, not learning in the outside world. I learned about private clients, billable units and the pressure of running a business. In the police force Mark learned about stress and danger, and seeing people at their best or worst.

Even worse, though, is what a lack of experience does to an MP. It turns politics into a game to be won, not dissimilar to chess or Risk. This can lead to a culture of game-playing and hanging around the press gallery trading gossip. At its worst, it involves briefing and leaking. And rather than politics being a contest of vision, values and ideas, for the new technocrats there isn't much difference between the political parties. For them, it's often good enough to fight over who can execute the same stuff best – leaving competence and ability to implement as the only things separating Labour and National. This is a cynical and sterile view of politics that I will never go along with.

This isn't simply a National Party problem. All parties seem to suffer from it, and it's international as well: in the UK there is a culture of 'PPE MPs', referring to those who left school, did a Philosophy, Politics and Economics degree from Oxford or Cambridge, then got into a minister's office and, before long, a safe seat.

New Zealand needs people who've done the hard yards, who've seen a little before they come to parliament, and who actually add something fresh and different to the place. Not technocrats in a game, whose main value is winning, right or wrong. Meanwhile, the rest of New Zealand is at the beach.

9
EDUCATION

OUR EDUCATION SHAPES OUR IDENTITY AS POWERFULLY AS almost anything. After our parents, it's the biggest formative influence for most kids these days, right from when they're toddlers in a child centre. As adults, the decision of whether we enjoy a lifelong interest in nature or in the New Zealand Wars, will probably have come from what happened in the classroom. Teachers and classrooms form us.

While there are always the exceptions to every rule – the college dropout who starts Microsoft, for example – most often your education is a predictor of success whether financially or in your health. There is a crystal clear correlation. More than that though, a quality education will enrich your life in intangible ways we may not be able to measure, but which are there sure enough, providing you with lifelong interests and passions for a good life.

My paternal grandparents, Naku and Alf Bridges. She was a kind, humble soul and he was a hard man, who treated her more like a servant than a partner.

Aunty Lorna and my grandmother Naku Bridges. Naku was clear to Lorna and my dad that the Māori world wasn't for them. This is how my siblings and I grew up as well.

My mum and dad, Ruth and Heath (left), and Dad's older sister, Lorna (right).

With Mum as an infant in 1976. I was two-and-a-half months premature and only three pounds three ounces at birth.

Dad, Mum and us six kids on our couches in the lounge, where we would watch the six o'clock news every night. I'm the baby in my mother's arms.

Me as a little guy, growing up in the late 1970s in Te Atatū Peninsula, or 'Tat North' as we called it.

With Dad at Footrot Flats Theme Park, Te Atatū Peninsula in the mid-1980s. It's a rare day out for just the two of us. Dad, as in this photo, never showed physical affection and always wore a collar and tie, no matter what.

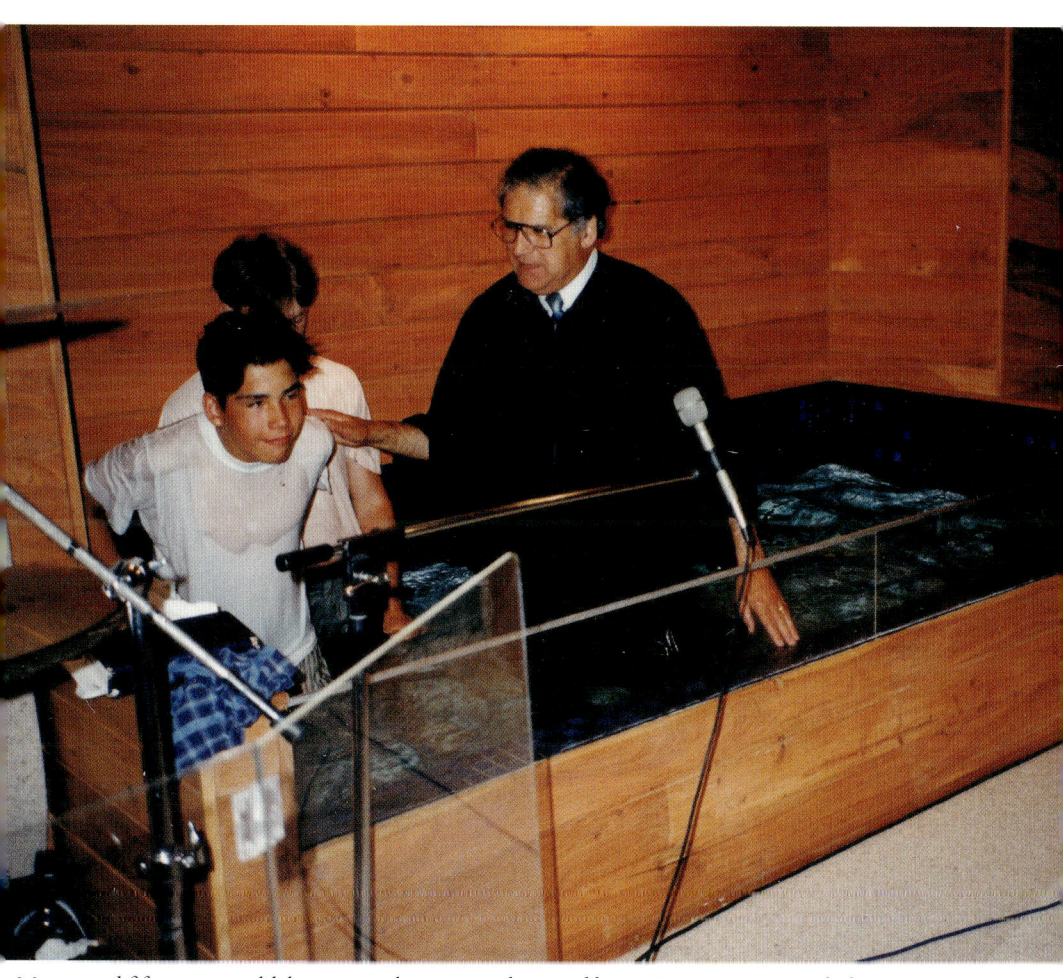

Me around fifteen years old, having just been water-baptised by my Baptist Minister dad in 1991. I learned to play drums on the drumkit in the foreground.

Eating shellfish on Christmas Day, early 1990s, at a fancy restaurant that Aunty Lorna paid for. My gout means I don't get away with eating crustaceans anymore.

On Santa's lap when I was a waiter at the Auckland Club in the late 1990s. This was the job that taught me how the other half live.

With Dad and Mum at the Auckland High Court on my admission to the Bar, 2000.

Discovering my English ancestry on a trip to Yorkshire in 2004. My family connection goes back at least several hundred years.

Natalie and I on our wedding day, 18 July 2005, at St Cross Chapel, Oxford, about a year after we met.

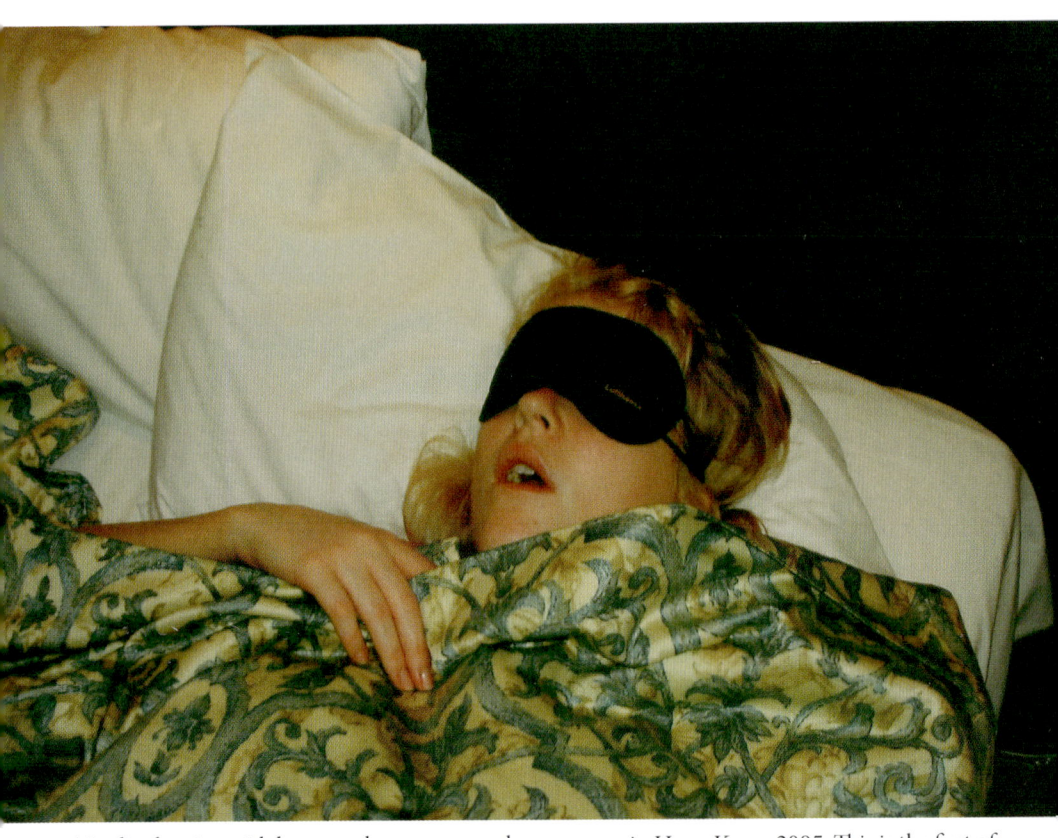

Natalie sleeping with her mouth open on our honeymoon in Hong Kong, 2005. This is the first of many pics I've taken of her asleep since we've been married – a recurring prank on her.

My family: Mum, Dad and us six children in the 2000s.

My first TV interview as MP for Tauranga, the morning after election day, Sunday, 9 November 2008, on our front lawn at Mount Maunganui. Natalie, my media advisor, watches on.

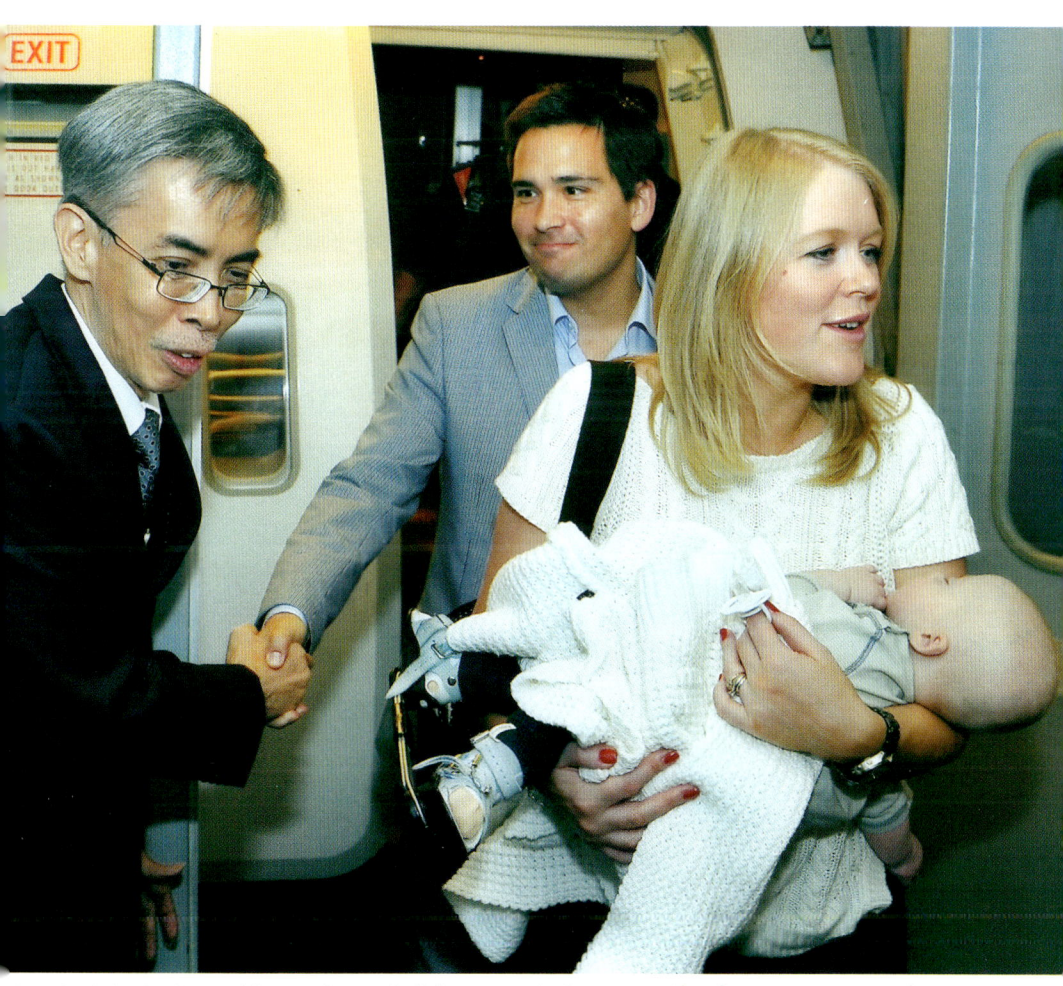

Natalie, baby Emlyn and I are welcomed off Singapore Airlines First Class by a government official, before being provided with a cavalcade to our hotel. I was there as a Lee Kuan Yew Fellow in 2012 and lived it up while I could.

At my happiest and most authentic as an introvert, reading in bed.

Whānau at my home marae in Oparure, King Country, 2009. Next to me with the walking stick is my dad's cousin, former Labour Cabinet Minister Koro Wētere. Growing up, we would cheer for him whenever we saw him on the news.

With our children, Emlyn (left), Harry (right) and baby Jemima, while I was leader of the National Party. Dressed up and about to perform at a regional National Party conference in 2019.

And it's not just at the individual level that education is transformational. For a nation, I believe it is too. Do it with excellence and produce a wealthier, healthier nation with a stronger scientific and cultural life, more inventions, patents and start-ups. Do it less well and be, well, a mediocre also-ran, following other nations.

My love of education and more specifically my lust for knowledge has always been so. From a very young age I remember trotting and then biking down to the Te Atatū Library just to be there with the books. I developed a love of libraries and books, how they look, smell and feel, but most of all what is in them. I remember talks with librarians there, I remember when I had been in the library all day and some bastard stole my HMX bike. From Te Atatū library I graduated to the central Auckland and university libraries. What a privilege it was to acquire knowledge not simply for an essay or assignment, but purely for the raw joy of it. My style at varsity, as it is now, was: if I was interested in something, to read not one but several books on the topic, to luxuriate in it. And if I could I'd sometimes buy the book, because then, in theory, I am storing the treasure, able to go back to it whenever I feel like it. That book's knowledge becomes mine, not temporarily but permanently. Books are like diamonds and diamonds are forever.

My father and his mother before him were possessed by the belief that education was the way to unlock a better future. To me, it's a means to something even higher: knowledge and wisdom, and therefore power.

Education in New Zealand is in crisis today. But the most worrying thing is that the majority of parents don't realise this. It's not like a big car crash, where the disaster happens instantaneously, as do the tragic consequences. In our education system, the tragedy — for that's what it is — is a slowly unfolding omni-shambles started over twenty to thirty years ago.

Two massive consequences from this shit's creek need to be understood before I get into what and why. First the inequality gap, the difference between the educational haves and have-nots, is worsening. I fear it's no longer a gully as it has always been, but a canyon. In its way, along with our nation's housing debacle, it has the potential to ruin us individually and as a body of people because it's not just an educational inequality. It goes, like housing, to real inequality and substantive poverty. When I started school nearly forty years ago, at an average, maybe a bit below average, primary school, it was still possible for someone to reach their potential at any school in our country, whether as a mechanic or as a surgeon. I don't think that's true anymore.

I said in my maiden speech at parliament how grateful I was for our first-class health and education systems growing up, and how important it is that governments red and blue continue to deliver in these areas. I fervently meant it. We can't give up on this and the ideal of equal opportunity for every single child.

There's a documentary on Netflix called *The Surgeon's Cut*. The first episode tells the story of a world-class obstetrician from Cyprus, now in London hospitals, who revolutionised certain procedures for foetuses in utero so that today many more babies live. The guy is now old and fighting his own health battles; his big eyebrows speak of his big brains. He is a living legend with God-like powers in the operating theatre of life and death. I believe that if we have a kid in New Zealand who could become an equivalent of this London Cypriot guy in thirty years, then that's what our schools have the responsibility to ensure – no matter gender, ethnicity or upbringing. Surely this is a core aim of an education system, allowing a child to reach the heights of their dreams. In the past we all had the boring basics drilled into us so we could go on to use that knowledge in more specialised endeavours, whether fashion design, mechanics or, yep, surgery.

But surgery requires serious mathematical and scientific, not to mention English, knowledge even before the kid gets to university. And with the changes that have occurred in the education system since I was a child, I don't think that kids from schools with the poorest demographics in my electorate or round this nation still get the shot they deserve. Raw ability and talent don't only come to rich kids, but opportunity through excellent education and achievement I fear increasingly does. And, tragically, that has a disproportionate effect on the poor and brown.

The NCEA data says I am wrong and everything is great. But sadly, that's not what the independent work from overseas makes brutally clear. The OECD's New Zealand testing shows we have the strongest link between socioeconomic background and how we go educationally out of all other OECD English-speaking countries. Like I say, good luck if you're poor and brown. You had a shot in the past to reach your potential. Tragically, not so much today.

The second consequence of our shit's creek is that, even for the kids from our middle and upper classes who have traditionally compared well internationally with those we think good – like Australia, the UK or France (let's not even mention developed Asian nations, who are now leagues ahead of us) – we are slowly, surely falling further behind. As education researcher Briar Lipson puts it, through the 2000s 'all major international assessments of pupil performance – PISA, PIRLS and TIMMS – have charted New Zealand's decline to educational mediocrity'. Some kids from those middle- to upper-class families and the higher decile schools they attend, of course, will still become surgeons or rocket scientists; but even then they won't be as good as those from other countries statistically. We are falling behind not just at the bottom end, but more generally now as well.

What's so concerning to me is, yes, most Kiwis don't seem to appreciate this is happening, and worse, I am not sure that many Kiwis would care. 'Oh well,' they say. 'As long as they are good kids who socialise well and can kick a ball, that's fine. And anyway,' they say, 'we can just import the skills and the specialisations and so on. I just want my kid to be happy.' Of course we all want our kids to be happy. But those who feel this way, I believe, are really accepting that we will become a country of second or third place, or worse. We will be a nation where we still farm and do tourism and build (very expensive) houses and where people aspire to owning a Ford Ranger and a boat. But the medical excellence, the Xeros and the Rocket Labs of this world will be elsewhere.

If the trend keeps on keeping on as it will, if we don't significantly change course, we will be Aotearoa New Zealand, nation of good lifestyle but not excellence. There's a global race on, and we will either be well back in the race or not even on the starting line. As for what's actually gone wrong, I reckon if you think about what I am saying and then look at your own education if you're under thirty, or your family's if you're older, you'll recognise it. Succinctly put, some years back New Zealand embarked on an educational experiment in its curriculum, and has continued to become more and more educationally complacent.

Before I am stoned by the educational fraternity, because we all know that criticism of our teachers is about as popular as crapping in the middle of the Sistine Chapel, I am not critical of teachers. I come from a family of teachers: my mum, her mum, my brother, my sister. Teachers are, as we all know, overworked and underpaid. Worse, they're at the mercy of fancy ideas – ruinously bad ones in fact – propagated around parts of the Western educational establishment and which sadly seem to be the dominant way of thinking in our own Ministry of Education.

The modern pedagogy, as these educational illuminati call it (always be distrustful of lofty jargon), includes three or so big ideas which sound nice but which ultimately, when put into practice, are terrible. American academic ED Hirsch summarises it like this: we've fallen into naturalism, individualism and the myth of generalised skills.

Naturalism is the idea, as expressed by the great Italian Marxist Antonio Gramsci, that 'a child's brain is like a ball of string that the teacher should help to unwind.'[2] The idea comes originally from philosopher Jean-Jacques Rousseau, who thought that if only we left a kid alone, they'd flower and flourish on their own. However, as Gramsci also said, 'In reality, each generation educates and forms each new generation. Education opposes the elemental biological instincts of nature; it is a struggle against nature, to dominate it and produce the "up-to-date" person of the new era.'[3] In plain English: quality education doesn't just happen for kids by letting them roll around on the floor. It's bloody hard, skilled work to teach and learn maths or a new language. It doesn't come easy.

Individualism is an allied thought, because teaching has to be tailor-made to the individualised needs and styles of each child (which will always be true to an extent). And I suppose a cousin to this is localisation, so that the curriculum must fit the context and needs of the child's region rather than be a blanket body of knowledge to be taught across a country. The big problem today is kids all over New Zealand learn different stuff. Education on this basis becomes a lottery, based on who you get teaching you where. You might be lucky, but in poorer schools particularly, you might not.

Finally, I'll touch on this 'skills' nonsense, where we now must 'facilitate' the learning of nebulous competencies instead of actual facts and knowledge for the twenty-first century. The trendy view is that the world is changing so fast that there is no point trying to know what we need to know in the future. On this basis, no longer are teachers actually teachers; they are facilitating kids to do whatever they feel like – so-called child-led learning – with the children picking up skills in the process. Don't take only my word for it. University of Auckland Professor Elizabeth Rata makes clear that today we no longer know if a particular school in, say, Taihape, teaches nine-year-olds about New Zealand poets, or poetry at all, or about 'our main towns, mountains and rivers', for example.[4] A localised curriculum means they don't have to teach anything substantive, really. Individual schools and teachers decide content. Some may do a great job; others not so much.

Secondly, given how education is now all about competencies, as Rata goes on to say, children miss out on knowledge generally. And third, regarding the individualisation of curriculum, 'student interest drives the pick and mix selection of supermarket education. But how do you know what you are interested in if you don't first know what it is? Interest follows from knowledge, it doesn't precede it.'[5]

I remember Mrs Reid at Rutherford High teaching us *Hamlet*. I would never have learned Shakespeare's *Hamlet* off my own bat, but it was in hindsight wonderful; his soliloquies are still capable of moving me. Now, though, teachers are encouraged to let each kid choose the book they want to read. As Briar Lipson in *New Zealand's Education Delusion* says:

> This approach rendered teaching the whole class impossible. Teachers could no longer read aloud to their class because each child was studying a different book. They could no longer ask the same pointed and pertinent questions that made their students think, or host class discussions that encouraged all students to participate. Even if teachers had super-human powers to read all the books and then plan and deliver

multiple lessons, an hour's class would only afford each child two minutes of teacher input.[6]

The reason behind this absence of core standardised knowledge is expanded on by Hirsch:

> Teachers have been told that subject matter is secondary, that they can teach strategies just as well with *Tyler Makes Pancakes,* or *Stupendous Sports Stadiums* as with a biography of Abraham Lincoln. This emphasis on technique at the expense of building subject-matter knowledge in early grades produces students who at age seventeen lack the knowledge and vocabulary to understand the mature language of newspapers, textbooks, and political speeches.[7]

This surely makes obvious how inequality in education is growing here, given this is how we teach our mokopuna — without consistency. I am sorry to the great teachers in our hardest schools. We know who misses out the most from the public system; who gets the roughest deal. Those from the lowest socioeconomic suburbs and towns almost inevitably do.

Every adult remembers a teacher or teachers who made a big difference in their lives. At primary school I remember Mr Vadner. He was tall and quite young and from Holland on some sort of teacher exchange. I also remember that he smoked, and this was very intriguing to me as an eight-year-old. Other than the principal, Mr Vadner was the only male teacher I had at primary, and this made me a bit scared of the big man. But scary or not, Mr Vadner did one remarkable thing for me that no one else had been able to. He taught me times-tables. Before this, I had become weirded out by multiplication and division and felt I would never be able to do them. Then came Mr Vadner for one year. He taught times-tables at the front of the classroom by rote, and each week or so he would expect us to have memorised, say, our six times-tables by repeating them again and again. A sort of name-and-shame system operated, where he would randomly call us up one-by-one to say them. Well, the combination of traditional learning and fear and loathing worked a treat, and today I am still a times-table champ.

Another great teacher was Mrs Butcher. She wasn't one of the cool teachers, far from it. Mrs Butcher was an older, plumpish, Pommie economics teacher. Her style was incredibly unfashionable even back then, some thirty years ago. You see, she also taught by rote and repetition. But how I learned. I devoured Economics 101 from a standardised set of notes that were impeccable in their explanations and analysis of supply and demand, economies of scale, opportunity cost, inflation, interest rates and more. Mrs Butcher's style of teaching real knowledge on real academic subjects is what we need to see in primary and secondary schools, even sometimes by rote and repetition.

And be clear, Mrs Butcher was by no means a stick in the mud. I remember once she was teaching us something like the economic law of diminishing marginal utility. It involved her getting me up to the front of the class and giving me Moro bars to eat. The first bar got a satisfaction mark from me of ten out of ten, the next was an eight. By the third or fourth, the grade was down to an appreciation level of about six, until by the fifth I would have paid to stop eating the bloody dreadful things. Teachers such as Mr Vadner and then Mrs Butcher prepared me very well for assessments and life after school. How quaint such old-fashioned lessons and examinations sound today.

Real academic learning doesn't need to be dry, but it should be a bit more than helping little Shamelia look up social media celebrities on Google and calling that a skill for the twenty-first century. My view is that the fad for giving our young lots of screen-time only guarantees one thing. Kids are becoming less and less likely to read in a sustained manner and less and less able to concentrate on traditional knowledge learning, which will be every bit as valuable a commodity in the twenty-first century as it's ever been.

When you think of a classroom, I am sure you picture a room for twenty or so children with a teacher at the front actually teaching. The reality today is very different: think of a long warehouse-like structure possibly for sixty, seventy, and maybe even more kids. Informally, the Ministry of

Education makes the schools get these structures if they want to obtain any actual funding

When I have visited these cow sheds, you'll have teachers and aides wandering around, maybe engaging and facilitating, while kids 'learn' as they wish. Some will be making scones (I have seen this), some will be on the internet 'researching' the latest Nintendo game or YouTube star (I have seen this). There may also be a bit of learning as I would recognise it (occasionally I have seen this). Teachers are trained nowadays not to talk too much from the front of a classroom. It's got to be child-led or group work.

Some of this modern learning may be okay, good even. I don't say it all needs to be old-style reading, writing and arithmetic, rote and repetition. But the pendulum has gone way, way too far one way. Schools should be about education, not daycare and socialising. The naughty kid who acts up because of what's happening at home, or the child with learning issues, they are slipping between the cracks. Out of a traditional learning situation they can be left to their own devices, lying on cushions daydreaming or looking up pictures on a screen.

Teachers will swear that this relatively new method and the cow sheds are amazing for 'socialisation', which is apparently so critical today, as if it hasn't always been. They may be right, and I grant it's a good environment for pre-schoolers, where socialisation is more important than formal learning. While on the matter of what works at different ages, I accept that self-directed learning comes into its own at high school, where students should already have core subject knowledge under their belts and so know where to start looking as they research, say, the sex life of the dung beetle. That said, even college needs to be supplemented heavily by teacher-led teaching from the front. Like Rata and Hirsch have intimated, if all you know to look for is cartoons from popular culture, you are never likely to investigate New Zealand poets, the history of Parihaka, the causes of the extinction of the moa, or party politics in New Zealand for that matter. It's a crisis in education, and the long-term ramifications for our wider society are terrifying. *Homo sapien ignoramus.*

In addition to what I've seen in many classrooms in the last decade as a politician, what's also had me hot under the collar is my and Natalie's experience with our kids. Our oldest was at a public primary school in his first year, and had a teacher that money couldn't pay more for. That's probably why she left the next year for more money elsewhere. After she left, our little boy went from thriving to stalling. The classroom seemed to be very culturally and socially astute, but we felt he was going backwards in maths, for example, a subject he had previously enjoyed. He was also going nowhere in other areas. We went and saw the school, who suggested we could afford after-hours tuition for core curriculum help. Natalie wasn't having it. Today, all three of our children go to a private school that teaches in traditional classrooms with small class sizes. Not NCEA, but the Cambridge curriculum. Now our son is over-performing, fully reaching his potential. I grappled with whether to include this fact because I know most people can't afford to do what Natalie and I have done. My parents, Ruth and Heath Bridges, certainly couldn't have; like so many others today, they couldn't even afford a house deposit when I was growing up. Neither could Natalie's parents.

I never ever thought I would send my children to a private school. I intuitively don't like the idea and want my kids growing up in a school that's as representative as possible of the communities we live in and are a part of. Ultimately, though, looking out for my kids is my top priority and trumps any prejudices or political views that I or, for that matter, anyone else might have.

What's interesting from watching my kids go to private school is that they don't go in cow sheds or do child-led learning. There is some of it, to be sure, but the style is much more traditional and subject-led by a teacher at the front of a classroom. Could it be that this is not only what the marketplace of parents want, having done their homework and being prepared to fork out a lot of money, but also because it's simply what works?

What I've also noticed about private schools is that, while some parents are rolling in the green stuff, many –

perhaps over half – certainly aren't. I've seen parents pick up their children in supermarket uniforms. Often they are new immigrant New Zealanders who place a premium on education and intuitively know that the national public system today is so variable, so they aren't mucking around with their children's futures. What's more, because oftentimes these parents weren't born here, they have experience of the big bad world we live in. They understand the value of getting to the starting line of the global race for talent in the best shape.

I predict that if we stay the course on our Kiwi educational experiment, private school rolls will continue to grow, and more New Zealanders will want better curriculums than the state system can deliver. In other words, regrettably and avoidably, a two-tier system will become entrenched – a bit like economy and business on an international flight, except if you're seated in the economy class of our education system, you may not even reach your desired destination in the future.

Another trend I am seeing among the rich and 'elite' in New Zealand these days is that kids, when they've finished school, skip our tertiary providers straight for overseas universities in places such as Melbourne or Sydney. In the past, the best of the best academically may well have gone on to a post-grad degree at another university offshore – but now some students are not even starting here. Of course, part of the reason is a more globalised world. But my clear conviction is that this also shows the decline of our universities, at least relatively speaking.

International score cards or rankings matter, and we keep slipping further behind. Soon enough, if we don't lift funding for Auckland — our only university still in the top hundred universities globally — then it will slip into the second hundred. By way of contrast, the 'seven sisters' elite universities in Australia are all top one hundred, with Melbourne in the top fifty, quite simply because the federal government over there keeps boosting their funding. China is also worth mentioning. Many an older Kiwi would never comprehend a Chinese university as being elite, but in the global educational arms race they have pumped in the investment and seen a result. Now two of the top thirty, and by some standards top twenty, universities in the world are in China.

As National leader, I set a goal of getting one of our universities back into the top fifty rankings internationally. Most colleagues didn't see the point in this, and in that regard they're probably like many New Zealanders. Only Paul Goldsmith and I, the so-called educational elitists, were proponents of the idea. I see it as pretty straightforward. We can slip comfortably, complacently, into a lifestyle country and nothing else; or we can keep fighting to compete in the world every so often. Having a top university and the ecosystem it fosters is critical if we want to maintain that aspiration at any level. The Americans, Chinese and our cousins the Aussies get it. Why don't we?

Realistically, it is about funding. Even more honestly, it's about having the courage to move away from a bums-on-seats model to a scenario where we unleash one or a small handful of varsities to charge more, and so be closer to world-class in certain specialisations. Some won't like this, but it won't mean kids miss out on getting a degree. It's simply that the quality spectrum would open up at the excellence end of the continuum.

It's not, despite my railing, too late. Certain schools, principals and teachers, tertiary providers, their administrators and academics, have held out. That's partly why we haven't declined further. And the UK example is very heartening. Their Education Minister from a few years back, Michael Gove, was intent on changing from the system we have in New Zealand today to a knowledge-rich curriculum and style where teachers lead. His leadership and teachers turned the ship around so that international scores are already recovering from an earlier steady, slow decline just like ours. Let's not slip inexorably into Aotearoa New Zealand, lifestyle (only) nation. Let's ensure that whether you're an orphan from the toughest suburb or the child of millionaires attending King's College, we have an education system that allows you to fulfil your God-given potential.

10
CRIME

SOME PEOPLE GROW UP FASCINATED BY CRIME AND DEVOUR novels, miniseries and true life stories on it. I was never like that. I didn't particularly like criminal law at university. That said, like a bee to nectar I was drawn to court work and especially the pinnacle of courtroom drama: the jury trial.

I started legal work as a junior litigation lawyer at the firm Kensington Swan, and I enjoyed it. But if you thought litigation meant doing court work, you'd be wrong. Modern litigation involves paper and large sums of money: most, actually nearly all of the time, it involves settlement before court, because to continue an argument in court costs too much. I remember one case I worked on as a very junior lawyer, at the end of each week delivering a cheque for $60,000 to the QC leading for us. This was twenty years ago or more, and he was only one (albeit the most expensive) of several lawyers on our side of the dispute. If you're a client, that's 60,000 reasons' to stay out of court, which explains why civil matters so rarely go there.

At Kensington Swan I did do some court work, but if lucky, it might be an hour a week arguing some matter of process or such like. While there I did only two criminal matters, the only criminal defence work I've ever done given that once you work as a Crown prosecutor you aren't allowed to act for the defence against the Crown. Both cases involved sentencing young men with rich client dads. In the first, the kid was caught by the coppers doing 160 kilometres up Parnell Rise – what a naughty boy – and in the second, it was an excess breath alcohol charge. In both, I rambled on to the judge about how the chap was from a good family and wouldn't do it again. Both got reasonably lenient outcomes.

But if I wanted to be a real Perry Mason, I needed to prosecute. Defence was an option, but in defence work as a young buck, you don't tend to be surrounded by good, significant lawyers who'll teach you well. More likely you'll be a baby barrister learning bad habits, destined for a life of drudgery on list courts pleading for Jimmy to get his limited driver's licence after losing it. Not exactly glamorous. In order to get senior and serious, and to one day do the sex, drugs and violence trials, I knew I would only get the pukka training and mentoring in a Crown Solicitor's office.

The problems were that the Auckland Crown firm, Meredith Connell, never advertised jobs and I had no contacts there. More to the point, while they may fairly disagree, my perception back then was that they wouldn't really be interested in a Westie Māori. Uncle Rupert or Aunty Priscilla had to be a judge. Today it's a PC United Nations; not so much back then. But then one day, 18 May 2001, in the Auckland District Law Society news, I saw it. An advert for an 'exciting opportunity' involving 'Court appearances on behalf of the Crown on sentencing and interlocutory matters, criminal defended hearings and jury trials' in Tauranga. Bingo.

I interviewed, got the job (for considerably less pay than I was on in Auckland), bid my central Auckland flatmates – who all thought I was mad – adieu, and I was prosecuting. I worked like a demon, and before long started doing jury trials under the supervision of more senior lawyers.

The trial work started at the most minor end: a defendant can elect jury trial for an offence with a three month or more prison sentence attached, and that covers a lot of crime, from theft right up to murder. Soon enough I had my training wheels off and was doing trials day after day by myself, accused and their counsel, a judge and a jury of twelve men and women, mostly good and true. Some weeks I could do a different jury trial every single day – cannabis cultivation, then male assaults female, then use of a document, then aggravated robbery, rounded out by assault with a weapon. I'd go home broken and exhausted. Unlike my life in Auckland, *not* being in court became more of a luxury than being before a judge.

But it was a tremendous way to learn. If Malcolm Gladwell's theory that you need 10,000 hours of practice on something to become a pro holds any water, I was getting there, and quickly. While it was tiring, the early days were a hoot filled with a lot of shits and giggles as I opened to juries, called witnesses, cross-examined accuseds and closed cases to the jury, sort of knowing what I was doing but also faking it till I made it. While not taking any crime lightly, especially where victims are concerned, the stakes were oftentimes low. Sometimes, though, it's the least important cases you remember the most. I certainly recall in the early days a number of cases I took on because of their quirks, or an inimitable rule of life – the crazy shit people do.

One such case involved a cheeky young upstart who'd been pulled over and breathalysed in his boy racer mobile at Pilot Bay, Mount Maunganui. Clearly young Sammy had been on the piss and, given that the breath-testing was done only a few hundred metres from the police station, the constable left the young drinker's car where it was and drove him in the police car back to the station for processing. Something then happened, and so the constable left Sammy in the car as he went briefly inside for a moment. Sammy spotted his chance, grabbed the breathalyser from the police vehicle and started sprinting away, breathalyser in hand. After all, if you haven't spent the last few years pining to own your own breathalyser, you clearly haven't lived. In all honesty my theory is that he probably saw a chance for a trophy to show his mates. But anyway, the cop came out and valiantly put up chase. Sammy was caught and charged with theft of a breathalyser.

When Sammy was sober, he scrubbed up as a clean-cut kid – maybe your child or mine – and he decided with his fairly average lawyer that taking his chances with a jury on this was a much better idea than going before a judge alone. Heck, while the case was open and shut on paper, with a jury in charge you just never know your luck.

The fateful day of trial came. Before the jury I called my witnesses, the central one being the officer who'd dealt with Sammy. Then Sammy gave evidence. I recall a cocky little rooster whose story was that this didn't happen, despite his being caught red-handed. The case closed, and the jury went out to consider matters. Open and shut, I would have thought. An hour passed, then another. Then another and then another. About eight hours later, after I'd enjoyed spare ribs and a steak at the Tauranga Lone Star, as was my habit while waiting for juries in the evening, the judge called the case off. Clearly those twelve couldn't sort their crap out. Several months later we did the case again. My recollection is that Sammy was convicted and sentenced to community work.

On the subject of the theft of strange items, I also remember around this time the case of Serena. Serena was a kleptomaniac. Among the things Serena liked to purloin was medical equipment. Here, the case was that Serena had stolen an ultrasound device from when she went into hospital for her pregnancy check-up. As with a breathalyser, if you've never owned an ultrasound, you really are missing out. When hospital staff found the machine missing, police went to Serena's home and retrieved it, and funnily enough they found other medical equipment that clearly wasn't hers as well. Why have just one ultrasound when you can have your own medical practice?

A trial starts with empanelling a jury. Defence and Crown each get to challenge potential jurors – six each. I basically only challenged if the person about to be sworn in had serious previous convictions, which I thought would impair their ability to impartially decide. As I learned early on, if you challenge everyone with an historic offence or a drink-driving conviction, you'd be hard-pressed to get to twelve people.

This ultrasound case was memorable because defence counsel employed a curious tactic I'd not seen before and haven't seen since. Mrs Jones would walk up and take her seat in the jury box. Next, Mr Smith would, but he'd be challenged by defence. Then, Ms Hohepa would get through successfully, but Mr Singh wouldn't. Defence challenged every man walking through the court to the box. And as the twelfth juror came forward, we had ourselves an all-female jury. To state the obvious, my adversary clearly thought women would show a little sympathy to another woman, pregnant at the time of the crime and desirous of checking her bubba's progress in the comfort of her own home.

When the jury was out picking a foreman (still to this day the antiquated language used, even for a female jury), defence raised an admissibility issue. I wanted to lead 'propensity' evidence, as it's called, about all the other medical equipment found at Serena's house along with the ultrasound device. Her defence was that she wasn't stealing but borrowing; the fact that she had a shedload of other medical kit in addition to the device made this defence logically less plausible. Well, the judge knocked out my propensity evidence. I wasn't allowed to let the jury know about the other stolen medical stuff. He had reasoned that while it was undoubtedly probative evidence, it was also highly prejudicial to the accused. The jury might wrongly reason that just because she was a thief and had done something strikingly similar before, so she did this time. 'Once a thief, always a thief' is possibly common sense in the real world, but is not good judicial logic. My case was starting to look less strong.

I called my witnesses before the jury and showed that Serena had been at the hospital, then the machine had gone missing, and then it had been found not long after at her home without reasonable explanation. I closed my case and Serena elected to give evidence. My cross-examination was pretty ineffective. She just batted me off as breezily as she batted her eyelids. Defence and I then made our closing statements, and the Judge closed to the jury by making it clear the Crown lost if it couldn't disprove that she had only intended to borrow. I felt dejected – I didn't feel it had gone well. It was no great shakes, yet people shouldn't steal hospital property.

But then the all-woman jury went out to the jury room. They must not have actually sat down, because before us lawyers had even left the courtroom they were back in the jury box with a verdict. Literally, they'd taken less than one minute. The court official asked, did they have a unanimous verdict? They did. Did they find Serena guilty or not guilty? Guilty. The male defence counsel's stratagem of women treating another woman more kindly clearly wasn't a clever one. In this instance, they mustn't have approved of selfishly taking an ultrasound device so other mums in our public health system couldn't use it.

With time and more experience under my belt, the seriousness and length of the cases increased, and the stakes became much higher for all concerned. Increasingly the cases were for commercial methamphetamine, serious violence including murder and sexual assault, where those in the dock, if convicted, would spend a good decade or more in jail, and their lawyers were no longer of variable quality. They were very senior and often QCs. All of this increases the stress on a lawyer and the exactitude required. A wrong phrase in court – as I well know – could land one's conduct under the magnifying glass in the appeal courts. In this phase I continued to work very hard late into the night and often wake at 4 am to go through the transcripts of evidence from the day before and plan my evidence work or perhaps the closing to the jury.

Sexual assaults were, and I am sure still are, at epidemic levels in the Bay of Plenty. I found such cases difficult but the most rewarding, and in a sense I became the office specialist in this area. Sex case after sex case after sex case. I say such cases are the most rewarding. This is for several reasons. First and foremost the victim, or complainant as they are called before conviction, feel their pain so deeply and are reliant on you as 'their' prosecutor. In vulnerability they share with you the most awful thing that has ever happened to them and they want justice. It's difficult not to be emotionally involved, at least at some level.

But sexual abuse cases are also the most rewarding in a professional sense. To me, they are clearly the most challenging test of a courtroom lawyer's advocacy there is. Murder cases are said to be, and in a penalty sense are the ultimate. But, without in any way wanting to be glib about so serious a topic, my experience of murders – and I did a few such trials – is of cases that technically aren't as testing. Sometimes they are glorified assaults gone wrong. Prove murder's simple legal ingredients (or elements, as they're called) and you have your man. By contrast, sexual abuse cases rarely turn on the technical definitions. For a rape, the Crown must prove sexual connection, a lack of consent by the victim, and a lack of reasonable belief by the accused that there was consent by the victim. Generally that means the defence says it didn't happen or, more often than not, it did but was consensual.

I appreciate this is all disturbing stuff to be discussing so freely. Probably you have in mind a woman at home alone when an intruder breaks in and forces himself violently on her – and I have done such cases. However, those sorts of cases are very, very rare. Most cases are between people who know each other very well, oftentimes because they are or have been in an intimate relationship or because at some level, biological or not, they are family. In such cases, the need for skill and humanity as counsel really is of the essence. A strong case on paper may turn out to be weak in court if the complainant has a bad day or those around her let her down. Likewise, bad on paper can turn out incredibly compelling if you as counsel bring your best, and the best from those in court with you.

Moreover, cross-examining a rape accused was always the most significant moment in court for me, akin in its own way to a surgeon performing an intricate brain surgery. The stakes are enormous for all concerned and the need to get things pitch perfect, sometimes soft and light and sometimes rough and tough, is everything.

As a comparison, parliament has nothing on a rape trial. A few loose words in parliament and the wrong thing said might result in being turfed by Mallard. But who cares? No one I know. At trial, get it right and a victim and her whānau get the restoration and justice they've waited maybe years for. Get it wrong and it's a miscarriage of justice. From the accused's point of view, of course the stakes are also monumental. Rape carries a standard penalty in our courts of eight years in prison. Add in what are called 'aggravating factors' and penalties can go up from there all the way to twenty years.

In terms of the substance of the sexual abuse cases I've worked on, I could probably write a crime book. As a young prosecutor not long into it, I was encouraged to keep a trial diary. In among the hundreds of cases are a lot of sexual prosecutions, ranging from a pack rape I recall at a gang pad on the outskirts of Tauranga, to older men who grossly and premeditatedly abused the trust of those around them to hurt and rob children of their innocence.

One case stands out so that I will never forget it for all of my days. This isn't because of its seriousness: having prosecuted a brutal double murder that resulted in the fourth longest sentence in New Zealand at that time. I have been involved in worse. And it isn't because it was particularly graphic with images I will never forget; again, I have done those cases and seen chilling police photos of dismemberment and blood and guts. This case stands out both because of the remarkable story at its heart and because of the offender: Tony Douglas Robertson.

It was a fine December school morning in 2005. A little girl, five, and her big brother, seven, were walking not far to their local school, Maungatapu Primary. The school had been encouraging the kids to walk to school to gain independence. An eighteen-year-old man pulled up to the curb in a car to talk to them. He told them their mum wanted the little girl to go with him and that he had Christmas presents for her. The man didn't want the boy, just the girl.

They were not a hundred metres from the school when he drove off with the girl – quite clearly, in my view, to rape and murder her. A day or so before this abduction he had been seen looking over a cliff and into a cave-like area not far away from where he would take the girl, presumably planning a place to dump a body. On that morning, once he had the little girl in his car, the young man drove up into the hills to a rural Tauranga waterfall. He stopped the car, put her seat down and got on top of her. She began crying.

Fortunately, this little girl's big brother was smart. He ran into the school and quite literally sounded the alarm. The teachers immediately called the police and a huge manhunt was set in motion. There was no time to lose. On intuition, Sergeant Dave Thompson drove a bit out of town. He was alone in his vehicle and not that far off retirement. He pulled into the remote Kaiate Falls car park. One car was there. As Thompson approached, the young man was getting on top of the crying new entrant child. The young man got up and, as Thompson rang this in to other police, an awkward and dangerous stand-off ensued where the young man told lies again about how he'd found the girl and was trying to help.

Police cars swarmed in and, as an aside, so did my wife, Natalie, a young journo covering the story for the *Bay of Plenty Times* by following the police radio. The little girl was safe. Dave Thompson was a hero. The High Court trial involved me and my junior lawyer against a long-suffering defence barrister who had to do the best job he could for Tony Robertson. Robertson was up on a raft of charges including abduction, kidnapping and indecent acts on a child. We were in court for a week.

While I have many courtroom memories, this one was like no other. Robertson was animalistic. Like a cunning rat one minute, a ferocious tiger the next. He would yell and swear at me, the police in charge of the case and even the judge. It's the only time before or since that I have asked the judge to put the prison guards between me and the witness box as I cross-examined someone. Robertson's anger was so palpable I believed he might have jumped from the box onto me.

Many witnesses were called, but the little girl's evidence was the most poignant and powerful. I will never forget her saying matter of factly, 'When I was walking to school, he stole me.' The Crown case closed, and Robertson got into the box and lied brazenly from the moment he opened his lips. He was no fool; he had read the disclosure he was entitled to as defendant, then weaved a story around the police case.

Then I rose to cross-examine him. My first question as we set off on hours of battle began bluntly. 'Mr Robertson, can we begin by agreeing you are a liar?' I'd thought a lot about what I wanted to achieve. I wanted to get him off guard, for the jury to see his true character, with a light shone on what had really happened. My cross-examination achieved its purpose. It was very charged. He would yell, swear, stand up as if to lunge. My tactic wasn't pretty, but certainly was effective. Here we didn't have an innocent man, framed by police and just trying to help, as he would have it. We had a lying angry perpetrator. Open and shut.

When the jury returned verdicts, Robertson was found guilty on all charges and was remanded in custody. At the sentencing before the trial judge, I applied for a sentence I rarely, if ever, sought: preventive detention. This meant jail until Robertson could establish he was safe to re-enter the community. Based on the psychiatric and psychological reports, which forecast a likelihood of serious violent and sexual reoffending upon release, that could mean the rest of his life behind bars.

Tragically, in hindsight, the judge saw things differently. Robertson received a sentence of eight years in jail but no preventive detention. It wasn't a higher sentence because Sergeant Dave Thompson had got to him and stopped what was inevitably going to happen, so Robertson couldn't be sentenced for rape and murder.

Eventually the eight years ran out. At this point Natalie and I were notified of the release by our copper mate, and officer in charge of the case, Pete Blackwell or 'Blackie'. I'd wanted to know about Robertson's release, as it seemed to me he was dangerous and vengeful. Natalie was terrified. We upped our home security with panic alarms by our bed, especially for the long stretches when as an MP I was away from home. Both of us would see his face around the place only to realise it wasn't him. I remember seeing him at the Mount hotpools and was sure he was looking at me. It was, of course, some other guy. We knew one day we would read of his reoffending if it wasn't perpetrated on us. A child, a death, something.

We didn't have to wait long. Just a few months after his release, Tony Robertson murdered Blessie Gotingco on the

North Shore. Now finally he is behind bars, hopefully for good, because of his anger, his obsession and his evil. He is one of New Zealand's worst criminals ever.

I don't say this lightly. Even your gang leader or your fraudster on occasion has charm or some sort of code of right and wrong, even if warped. But Robertson, not at all. It was like his wiring was different or maybe not even joined up. He was an angry animal, thankfully now caged for good.

While I didn't realise it at the time, because of cases like Robertson's, by 2008 I was burnt out after several years of prosecuting. I had worked like a slave and gone from junior to intermediate to senior Crown counsel incredibly quickly. While still young and energetic, I was tired and more than ready for something new.

Day after day, early morning after early morning, evening after evening, I was seeing the worst of human nature and it wasn't much fun. I didn't know I was doing so until I left, but I internalised some of the darkness. You can't help it. Some inevitably rubs off. Yep, we prosecutors shared a lot of black humour to cope with what we saw, but the steady diet of child abuse, rape, violence and more child abuse really got to me. I wasn't the kind of person who could just brush it off in the weekend; I cared too much.

In a way it was like an addiction. The buzz was still there to some small degree, but nowhere near as good as it had been. The fun had gone. And I often wouldn't sleep, worrying, running over closing addresses and cross-examinations in my head, clear in my mind that Sarah or Mihi or Charlene needed justice and so I must get it perfect. I cared too much.

I know all this because when I decided finally to throw in the towel on prosecuting in exchange for a life in politics, a weight lifted physically from my shoulders. I felt it. Natalie also remembers it well, because suddenly I could sleep properly through the night without tossing and turning and waking to write down notes on my current trial. That meant she too could sleep better. By and large I have continued to sleep like a baby throughout politics in a way that, towards the end of my legal career, I just didn't.

Politics, perhaps against the common perception, has been so much more positive for me than law. In criminal trials I could potentially do justice for one victim and one whānau, slowly grinding it out case by case. But in politics, more easily than some imagine, you can change the rules of the game and achieve justice for many thousands. In politics, real lasting positive change is much more possible than in law. In my maiden speech I grandiloquently stated:

> Martin Luther King Jnr once said that injustice anywhere is a threat to justice everywhere, and in many jury trials I have seen injustices – indeed, manifest indignities – performed on the weakest in our society as court rules worked against them. We need to make law that redraws the balance between victim

and community on the one hand and criminal accused on the other. Victims and the community deserve better than the so-called justice I have seen served up to them on occasion, and although there has been tinkering previously, more reform is needed to make the jury trial a more just institution. In short, juries need to be trusted with more information, and victims need to be treated more evenly when compared with accused.[9]

I came in keen to be Minister of Justice one day, full of criminal law reform ideas, and in one of my first requests of John Key I sought to be on the justice and law and order select committees. However, John had different ideas, and as a minister I was much more focused on the economic and infrastructural spaces. It was only really as Opposition leader that I came back to justice, railing against soft-headed approaches by Jacinda and her crew (with good effect on National's polling), but also because I believed it and still do. Crime and gangs need a deterrent approach, not pussyfooting around.

As Opposition leader I saw for myself the exponential growth in gang membership. In Tauranga it became that you couldn't go out on the weekend, certainly not on the main drags downtown or at the Mount, without seeing Filthy Few, Mongrel Mob or Head Hunters parading themselves and their bikes. Knowing their form in our courts, I found this abhorrent. I put out a law and order discussion document. A staffer and I worked hard on it and I still believe it's a tremendous work of both policy and politics. I also began moving round the country doing public meetings and banging the justice drum. These forums and the messages in them were gaining real momentum until Covid-19.

I will never forget when, after some gang warfare early in 2020 that had frightened locals, I held a public meeting with the other local MP, Todd Muller, and my justice spokesperson at the time, Mark Mitchell. The auditorium we had chosen was packed and, amazingly, a number of patched and unpatched gang members came, as did plain-clothes police. Arguments between the Waikato Mongrel Mob spokesperson and me made the news, but one thing from the meeting not reported still makes me chuckle. Natalie was up the front row to watch and support me. She has always been a good egg like that, fiercely protective of me. Directly behind her was a Mongrel Mob member known to me, as I'd seen him round a bit, generally patched up. He was muttering about me when Natalie turned around and started to really go at him. He then promptly called her a bitch and it was all on; Natalie was really kicking off. I could see all this as I was about to begin the meeting. I walked over and told them to both be quiet and behave themselves. Neither spoke the rest of the meeting. Every so often the Mob and Natalie do listen to authority.

Today the gang problem continues to grow and grow, meaning inexorably more victims of crime and less public safety. I accept, as I always have, that the causes of crime are incredibly complex. I actually accept that among the many contributing factors are colonialism and institutional racism. I know from my own experience that people in authority can treat brown people differently to white ones. It would be naive to think otherwise. Yet, that does not excuse serious criminal behaviour. Two young men growing up on the wrong side of the tracks can both have every reason in the world to head into a life of gangs and crime, but one resists where the other doesn't. We must be more on the side of the one who resists. Every day, plenty of people with all the rationales in the world choose to do the right thing. There are no excuses for those who don't.

While university types will swear till they are blue in the face that a deterrent approach doesn't work, there is plenty of evidence it does – at least, better than the mollycoddling alternatives. If Johnny knows that he will get caught and sentenced, he's less likely to do the crime. And the next Johnny is too. And while the criminologists will also come for me, morally we also need to see a proportionate punishment for the offence – crime cannot pay – otherwise, at the extreme, people will take the law into their own hands. Again to pick on Johnny: if the tariffs for child abuse go too low, the child's family will – and I have seen this – go out and act as judge, jury and ... you get my drift.

It's not an either/or situation with tough on crime in one corner and 'Kumbaya' in the other. We need both. I am all for rehabilitation and reintegration, but it must go hand in hand with the meting out of justice. People are capable of redemption. As a Christian, I have to believe that. But it's not so effective while the person's still running with the gang, meth in one pocket and an illegal firearm in the other. Catch them. Bring them to justice to deter them and others. Then help them as best we can to never do it again. Set them up for a better life.

I got a lot of press and controversy early on in 2021 after calling Police Commissioner Andrew Coster a wokester with his softly, softly approach to law and order. Like me, I understand PC Coster is motivated by religious belief and that is a powerful thing. Unlike me, however, he believes coppers can be 'transformative' prior to conviction and jail for the serious stuff. Coster and others high up in government who think so naively have the cart before the horse. Police need to do their job, and arrest and bring before the courts. Only then is there room to connect rangatahi with their hapū and iwi, provide skills and training to those who need it, and offer mental health services to the unwell.

I've never been as fascinated by crime as some. But I am fascinated by people: the crazy shit we do, how we mete out justice for our safety, and transform people's lives for theirs and society's redemption.

11
FOOD

MUCH OF WHAT I REMEMBER FROM THE PAST I REMEMBER through food-memory – by remembering the food we enjoyed at the time. Oftentimes I remember it at the expense of the conversation, even the people I was with. That's the power of food.

I remember meeting my wife, Natalie, through the food we ate that night. I first talked to her at a formal college event at Oxford. It was dry sherry and fruit platters. I then took her a few days later on a date of sorts to a Singapore-style noodle joint. It was a terrible idea – such an impossible thing to slurp politely, and for me as a messy eater it was a double mission not to get it on myself. I don't think she ate much. On the walk back to college after, we got takeaway coffee from a little patisserie. I ordered a long black and then, not having put the lid on properly, spilled the boiling black liquid out one side of the cup onto my hand. That forced me to over-adjust so that I then spilled it out of the other side of the cup, burning myself again albeit on the other side of my hand. I then reflexively set about repeating those actions again and again. I burned myself quite badly but I suppose there was a glimmer of sunlight: it humanised me in the eyes of my now-beloved and created a sense of empathy for me, such was my haplessness. No regrets.

In addition to creating memories, food has always been my family's way of bonding. In good times and bad, like most families I'm sure, we eat together. Probably it's the one consistent thing I always did with family growing up, and the one consistent thing I do now with Natalie, Emlyn, Harry and Jemima. No matter what else is going on, we share dinner every night. It's a chance to talk and to eat, even if it is at 5.30 pm to suit the kids. Not exactly continental in its timing but again, no regrets.

Maybe as a consequence of our own focus, the kids are now all foodies. The boys love a cooking show, whether Rick Stein (my favourite), Jamie Oliver, *Cake Boss*, *The Great British Bake Off* or one of the many *MasterChef* series. And now they both cook (Jemima's still a little young). I remember Emlyn as a six-year-old begging to see Nigella Lawson when she came and spoke at the Auckland Town Hall. He even wanted to ask her a question: 'How do you become a good cook?' As for Harry, he is even more into it, and for a couple of years now has had a clear and unwavering plan to open a restaurant when he is older. He already has the name, and you probably won't find it hard to work out. Harry wants to call it *Harry's*.

When I grew up we didn't have much. I don't want to paint it as 'Simon Bridges, boy who grew up in a log cabin', the sort of background fable one wants to portray in order to become President of the United States. It was fine, good even; I didn't have any perception of poverty. But eight of us – four boys, two girls and Mum and Dad – lived on one small Baptist stipend in a rabbit warren of a church manse in Te Atatū. And we did fight for food.

Mum knew how to make a little go a long way and was by necessity tighter than a duck's sphincter. Nothing was wasted. Everything was grown, used and re-used. Much of our food came from her big garden and was seasonal. I remember a lot of spinach, corn, potatoes and peas at the right times of year. She would stew and preserve everything, from fruit that she got on special at the supermarket or produce store, to rhubarb she had cut from the garden. I remember loving strawberry picking with her out at Helensville. We'd eat our fill and then pay for what we'd managed to get into the bucket. We would then have these for dessert for a week or two, sprinkled with icing sugar, and she would use the rest for jam on our sandwiches in and out of season. Jam and other preserves went in any and every receptacle there was. A sister-in-law recently marvelled at a plastic container in the fridge containing some food item. Turns out it was previously a haemorrhoid cream tub. Old frugal habits born of necessity die hard.

Speaking of fruit on special, it was often from a seconds bin and ripe to within an inch of its life. More bruise than fruit. Mum would tell us they were the best bits. Now in more prosperous times, I've come to realise that fruit doesn't have to be so soft, juicy and dark to be enjoyable. That was Mum's way of tricking us to eat it. I think now, however, she's been doing it so long she's also tricked herself. Old habits, again.

Dinner time involved me walking around the house ringing a homemade bell with a key tied to it by a wiry old pipe cleaner. I would roam around the kids' rooms then down to the steel door of Dad's garage study, *ding-a-ling-ling-ling*ing. All would run up to the dining table and food would be there, bulk-made like a school camp and – I mean this as a compliment on your resourcefulness, Mum – of about the same quality. Good, but not exactly Michelin star. It couldn't be on Mum's budget.

I remember sausages with mashed potato, peas and corn. I remember roasts. I remember corned beef, mash and onion with white sauce. I remember pan-fried rice with Worcestershire sauce, peas and parsley from the garden, bacon pieces and egg. I remember pancakes, as per Delia Smith in the old English style, with lemons from the tree. I was allowed to help cook these and flip them, something Emlyn and Harry now enjoy. If we were being adventurous and they were going cheap, we sometimes put bananas in the mix. I also remember *Edmonds Cookery Book* pikelets. When the mix on the pan bubbled, I turned them over. We would eat them hot with butter and sometimes Mum's jam and cream.

As for any leftovers at mealtime, there would be a battle. In this it was an alpha male contest, like gorillas fighting in the Congo for supremacy. Dad was first child among seven and would fight for the next sausage, generally winning until the older boys were big enough to take him on. On that subject, I do remember, rare as they were, a fight or two at the table. One time there was some argument between Peter, the oldest, and Dad. Maybe Dad was throwing his weight around, perhaps he wanted the last sausage, and Peter by this stage was old enough to take him on, bear-hugging Dad so he couldn't move, he could only flap around like a leaf in the breeze. After that, Dad didn't muck around with Peter anymore. There was a shift in the power dynamics in the household. And in who got to eat the last sausage.

Another time Timothy, the next oldest, and Peter had a fight over some nonsense. One of them split their toe open on a table leg as they jostled for top primate position. The girls yelled at them to stop but the rest of us just sat at the dinner table and watched.

Given the slight scarcity of food, as a youngster I learned to eat fast. That way you had a stab at getting more. This didn't just apply to dinner time. Say there was a packet of Arrowroot biscuits – you'd want to eat as many as you could so they were mostly yours. Otherwise another brother would eat them. Chocolate biscuits and you'd go for your life.

On Friday nights we might once in a while have fish and chips. We wouldn't buy the fish from the takeaways, as Mum got that cheaper elsewhere, but we lived less than a hundred metres from the Golden Eagle Takeaways on Gloria Avenue, Tat North, and I would be sent over to get a couple of dollars of chips – a lot in those days. I would enjoy my little expedition, handling money and interacting with the Chinese people who worked and owned the shop. The man would sometimes ask me if I was Chinese and I would always tell him, no, part Māori. He was just picking up on my Cliff Curtis crossover quality, where someone with a little Māori can play a Mexican druglord or an Asian warrior (as I once did, as an extra in *Xena: Warrior Princess*).

For school lunch, Mum would make me sandwiches and give me fruit. But once a year on my birthday, I could take a dollar and buy one Big Ben steak pie. Steak, of course, is the king of meat. The pies were kept in a pie warmer at the little temporary tuckshop set up during lunchtime in the school staffroom. They were lukewarm, I remember, so I could devour them very quickly. This meant I was always hungry after.

When I was in my last year of primary school, I remember being given the privilege of helping once in a while with the running of the tuckshop. The reward for this was the joy of eating the broken biscuits from biscuit packets when the bikkies were on sale. I remember secretly breaking them so we could eat more of the chocolate thins and fingers, which Mum never got for us at home.

When I turned fifteen, I began working at Foodtown (today called Countdown, for the youngies among you) in Te Atatū North, then South, as all my older siblings bar one had done before me. Over my illustrious career I went from plastic bag (Remember them?) packer to assistant grocery manager in the weekends, more than doubling my pay over five years from four dollars and five cents to nine dollars something. I don't think there was a minimum wage back then. Jim Bolger may be all Green Party left these days, but in the nineties he was what some call neoliberal.

At the grocery, I remember being out back, where the trucks brought in the products in cardboard boxes. We would then take what was there out onto the store shelves. Other staff would sometimes 'accidentally' slash the boxes with their Foodtown-provided craft knives. They'd do it in such a way that the packets of sweets and chips would also be cut and unsaleable. We would all then crowd around out back, eating these to our hearts' content. Forbidden fruit is the sweetest.

Even better were the stints I used to do in the delicatessen. Between weighing and serving old ladies their corned beef, salami, coleslaw and stuffed peppers, I would gorge myself on the open cheeses as well as strings of cocktail sausages with the supposedly cancerous red skin on them. Rows of the little bastards would slink down my gullet to my gut.

In hindsight, it might be here on Saturdays at Foodtown that I developed a lifelong weakness towards cheese and cold meats. Though before this I do also remember, as an eleven-year-old-boy at my big sister's wedding reception, being introduced to this new thing: the Cheeseboard. Life prior to this had been all Colby and Tasty. Don't get me wrong – I still, along with Edam, enjoy these common varieties. At Rebekah and Roger's wedding reception, though, there were all manner of fancy numbers – the brie, the camembert, the gouda, even the blue. And because Roger's dad was on the New Zealand Dairy Board and had provided so much, I was dining out on the good stuff for weeks after the big day.

So food-life growing up wasn't all school camp. There was the odd high point every now and again. One person deserves special mention for their starring role in my siblings' and my culinary journey: Aunty Lorna, Dad's slightly older sister. As a young woman, she had moved from New Zealand to San Francisco and stayed there for the rest of her working life before returning to retire at Stanley Point in Auckland.

Because she had no kids of her own, when she came home to visit once every year or two, we would be spoilt.

This spoiling wasn't just limited to when she came home. Every birthday we would receive massive boxes from the US with the most weird and wonderful presents a Kiwi kid could imagine. You see, Aunty Lorna was crazy in a good way. She was more flamboyant and different than anything you got in beige old New Zealand those days, dressing with colour, patterns and prints, big earrings and necklaces, often multiple at once, wigs and loud make-up. Her get-up was stuff she had brought in the Amazon and Africa, at Gucci and at a garage sale. She definitely had a distinct aesthetic going on. The boxes contained whatever the latest California craze was, from rollerskates to colour pens, cartoons and underpants emblazoned with the Incredible Hulk, Superman or Batman. In an age before mass production from Asia, she blinged us out and opened our eyes in a way other kids never knew.

When she would visit us in Auckland, we would do something we never ever did at any – and I mean *any* – other time, growing up. Aunty Lorna told Dad we could all go to any restaurant anywhere in Auckland and eat anything we wanted from the menu. Well, my dad wasn't too proud to take his much wealthier sister up on this. And so I recall in the 1980s, when there just wasn't even a per cent of the restaurant range and volume we see today, living it large each time Lorna visited. We went to Tony's Steakhouse, the Sheraton, the Hyatt, Langton's at the top of Mount Eden, and others as well. I recall soft drinks, crispy potatoes and meat. I also remember crayfish, snapper, mussels, and this fancy sauce called tartare. The eight of us ate all we could. Thank you, Aunty Lorna.

Possibly these restaurants weren't the best in Auckland at the time – not in a strict sense. But we picked them because we knew of them, and I feel like they all had a buffet, which would have appealed to us hugely at the time – a chance to eat fast and as much as we could, and to really get our (or Aunty Lorna's) money's worth. Today, going to a restaurant might not seem like quite such a big deal, but back then, wowee! Now that I eat out several times a week, the treat for me is probably in reverse, eating at home. How times change.

Sadly, once I had the habit of fighting for food and an all-you-can-eat mentality, it was hard to shake. Deprogramming isn't that easy. As a young person I was a bit of a rake, physically speaking, lean through my school years. However at university, with a bit of drinking I got properly porky. One of the other factors was my hospitality work. At the Auckland Club, and then at other cafés and bars, I was often working evenings and then off to lectures first thing the next morning. I recall working through to midnight, then in the kitchen eating leftover lamb shanks and mash or chicken breast and chips till I could pop. The food in abundance gave me energy for my lack of sleep and rest, but resulted in me getting heavy.

When university finished I realised I had to put a stop to this. I began running. Every day, half an hour. That became an hour and, after a while, I was regularly running half marathons and the odd marathon. I then managed to stay relatively slim until kids, Cabinet and middle-aged injuries slowed me down. As a young professional I also began eating better. Girlfriends and then Natalie introduced me to a wider world than fast-eating in bulk. I somewhat – and I emphasise only somewhat – reprogrammed to smaller, higher-quality portions.

Nevertheless, today my dad bod is heavier than it should be. I don't have a massive number of excuses other than living and eating well, with more-regular-than-they-should-be binges on cheese, meat, red wine and single malts.

One thing I can no longer eat – despite occasionally letting myself down and regretting it – is any sort of crustacean. Oysters, which I adore; scallops, which I crave; and crayfish, which I covet – all contain purines. And they, for a Māori male like me, not as fit as I could be, when washed down with beer or sauvignon, create gout. For the uninitiated, gout is a real shocker. I can remember the first time it struck, thinking I must have somehow badly sprained my ankle. One of them had swelled up badly, was hot to touch, throbbing and excruciatingly painful. I was also debilitated, unable to move, let alone walk around. I was a Cabinet minister at the time, and because I could barely walk I went to a doctor. She laughed and gave me the diagnosis. We also had the blood test for good measure, but sure enough my uric acid levels were through the roof. Garden variety, incapacitating, gout. The specific trigger for this gout was abundantly clear. A few days before with a close friend and our wives, I had been out to a Bay of Plenty lodge for a long dinner. It was a special occasion and the friend pulled out wonderful Kiwi and French wines, including some bottles of Dom Pérignon from the eighties. When we were well lubricated at the bar, we went to a private room for dinner. First round was scallops. I enjoyed them so much and the wine was so good with them that I ordered more, feasting on little taonga after little taonga. Then we had venison, as rich and heavenly as it can be, and I kept on drinking. I don't recall a lot after that, save for the fact that the owner of the place, a friend of my friend, came in at some point with a live baby deer that wandered around our dining room for a time as we shared more drinks. It was surreal, given the little one's big brother or parent had probably been our main. Very late in the evening, or rather early the next morning, we retired.

As bad as the gout from that occasion was, soon enough I forgot about it. My foot got better and, as Mike Hosking says, 'Happy days.' A couple of years passed and, again after drinks and shellfish, back came the dreaded ailment. Most recently I've suffered it terribly after a dinner with Natalie and the kids at Charlie Noble in Wellington, where I sought to teach Emlyn and Harry the joys of good oysters, and again not long after that when I foolishly shared a couple of crays with a friend at his restaurant. They were in abundance because of Covid and the inability to get them through to China at the time. Charlie Noble and then the crays forced a fateful decision. No more kaimoana, save for fish. Since I've given up crawling beauties from the sea, I haven't had gout. Long, good Lord, may that continue.

Lest you read this and think I am a Falstaffian gourmand about to fall to the ground and die, my doctor thinks I am in pretty good health and my exercise regime has picked up somewhat since my deposition as Opposition leader. I am still very much a meat eater, though less so today than has been the case in the past – not for any ethical reasons or in any bid to save the planet, but merely for my own humble diet and strength. At home I try to stick to porridge and fruit in the morning, though toast with peanut butter and marmite (on different pieces) does sneak in periodically. Lunch is often a salad. I try not to eat meat every evening.

While I drink alcohol regularly, I don't regularly drink much. A glass or two when I do drink, and days without often enough. That said, I do like a red and I do like to imbibe it with red meat.

One day I swear to my wife I will live out a couple of food fantasies. One of which I love for its romance and mysticism and the other for its crass contrarianism. In the former I have a longstanding dream to walk the Camino de Santiago across the middle of Spain. A university friend did once, leaving New Zealand overweight and pasty but coming back fit and tanned. More than that though, I recall him telling me a tale of enlightenment on this eight-hundred-mile ancient pilgrimage to St James's relics, of stopping in at villages every evening and staying in little bedsits while eating peasants' paella and quaffing tempranillo with fellow travellers. What could be better? It will happen.

My other food fantasy is one I have harboured for quite some time. While it may never happen, sometime I'd love to treat myself to a bottle of Pétrus, Pomerol and a couple of McDonald's Big Macs. The Pétrus wine from Bordeaux retails at about $6000 but I would do this with a 1982, which retails at about $12,000, as it is the year Natalie was born. I would probably let her have a glass (remembering that one glass is itself a couple of grand or more). As for a couple of Big Macs, they cost around $12. Despite the difference between them, both the red wine and red meat are world class icons in their own way and, I believe, a match that would be made in heaven.

I have been amused when I sometimes tell people of this lifelong ambition. I remember, for example, telling a small group of friends at a social gathering after we had had a few. While some laughed and bought into it, one woman there – wealthy, a wine connoisseur and a vegan – nearly choked on her lentils and eggplant. She was bloody horrified. I didn't know her that well, and Natalie reminded me afterwards that the woman had said earlier that she'd given up meat as an ethical decision. It was killing the planet, and giving it up was something meaningful she could do. If she didn't like red meat, she was bound to hate the golden arches. Politics and identity are to be found in food here in New Zealand like never before. This woman demonstrates it. To her, what she eats is an ethical and political choice, and statement about who she is. She is what she eats in a wider sense than physically. Those who do different to her are worthy of her judgement.

When you think about it, there is a politics of food. The left is reasonably obvious with its tofu and kale juice; the right is probably meat and three veg. Indeed, a centre-right politician the world over, maybe because of our agricultural bases, loves to be seen with meat. Pies, burgers, bacon, you name it. This is nirvana. Perhaps all of this ties in to how Green MP Chloe Swarbrick holds the most expensive, capital-of-kale suburb in our country today: Auckland Central. Politics and identity increasingly trump the more basic Maslowian hierarchical concerns, especially as you get higher up the hierarchy.

What the vegan at the social function also shows is that food and class are a thing. Her veganism is part of who she is, and that's okay by me. I wonder, though, if she realises that those with less wealth than your average Herne Bay Green voter would find it much harder to be a vegan – certainly to do it well. Regrettably, good quality and varied fruit and veg are expensive. Much more so than, say, your average mince (okay, basically gravy) pie these days. Let them eat asparagus, to paraphrase Marie Antoinette.

If I was to be unkind, I might say there is food snobbery. Açai berries, kale, organic, almond milk: these are now the stuff of the thin and wealthy. White bread, sugar, red meat, McDonald's: these are for the lower classes. I view food as more than a matter of politics or identity or a statement of my class. I see what I eat as a choice based on enjoyment and, as I age, health (no shellfish and less meat, more greens). It wasn't always this way. I doubt that thirty or forty years ago there was so much food self-consciousness. People ate whatever was in front of them, and I don't suggest that was perfect either. But undeniably as we've become more affluent, we are able to make it more complicated. So therefore many of us do.

To some, meat equals bad, yet it is simplistic to simply blame meat for climate change. Done efficiently, there are fewer carbon miles and more efficient farming in a lamb rack moving from the Wairarapa to London than there are from

Wales. Having been around these arguments for some time and having thought a fair bit about climate change, the real baddies are fossil fuels and primarily Old King Coal. Lamb and beef and all the rest are not the main issue, as China and India build coal plants quicker than I could drink that most excellent bottle from the Château.

What's more, the almond milk and the açai berries probably aren't squeaky clean. I am not bagging them, and if you eat them for taste or health, be my guest. I just ask that you don't do it with too much superiority. Almond plantations in California are said to be doing a world of environmental harm. Pick the plank (of kale) from your own eye before you worry about the speck (of salami) in mine.

As a major agricultural producer, do the trends in food politics count against us over time? Personally, I doubt it. For all the fashion and fads, and even technological advancements like synthetic and plant-based meats, I reckon there will always be enough people who want an actual beef steak or venison rack. Meat, my friend, isn't going anywhere.

12
MUSIC

MUSIC CAN BE A SPIRITUAL EXPERIENCE. COMPARE AND contrast any good modern pop or rock concert with a Pentecostal praise and worship time. They are almost identical. Hands are up, eyes may be closed, people are in a sense of heightened emotion and awe and adoration. Sometimes at rock concerts that's the drugs, to be fair. But with or without such external stimulation, music is capable of taking one higher into another realm.

Having grown up in a Pentecostal church and having gone to many a concert, I am familiar with both phenomena. Spiritual music is of course meant to be a spiritual experience, but at some level the non-religious stuff is too. I remember as a young kid watching some wacky religious videotape called *Hells Bells* (after the AC/DC song, I think). Its purpose was to scare the Jesus into you by showing demonic forces at play in 'the world's music'. It featured Fleetwood Mac band members high and out of their minds as they performed. And it went into great detail about the evils of backmasking, the satanic technique whereby sound and messages are recorded backwards into tracks that are played forward. Thus if you played one of my favourites, 'Another One Bites the Dust', backwards at precisely the correct speed, it would sing, 'Start to smoke marijuana, start to smoke marijuana'. Led Zeppelin's 'Stairway to Heaven' had Robert Plant saying, 'Yes, my sweet Satan. Yes, my sweet Satan.' Now I don't know exactly what was going on here – my best guess is some rockstars having a laugh in between a wee snifter of coke and a vodka tonic. But as a young 'un I was petrified. I can't recall if it was off the back of this videotape or some other Christian message, but I remember my older brothers burning their hard rock LPs in our outside fireplace. The entire collection of Kiss went up in smoke, and burning records make a lot of it.

In any event, I have always loved live music for the transporting effect it has on me. The first real concert I ever went to (okay, I went to Cliff Richard with Mum at the Logan Campbell Centre before this, but that really doesn't count) was U2's *Rattle and Hum* Lovetown Tour with BB King at Western Springs. I was twelve or so, and went with my older brother Mark. Weed wafted strongly through the air. From then on, the concerts flowed thick and fast. Through my teens I saw all the big alt-rock type acts: Pearl

Jam, the Red Hot Chili Peppers, Smashing Pumpkins, Rage Against the Machine.

I also remember Paul McCartney and Wings came to New Zealand, again at Western Springs. I can't recall who I was with, but we didn't have tickets and so paid, like, ten bucks to watch it from an adjoining home to the park. This was all very well but a bit limiting, and so about a quarter of the way into the concert someone put a ladder up against the wall and those game enough jumped then ran down the steep terrain into the crowd. I did likewise. Up the ladder. Look around. Jump and *faar*king run. Security guards would yell and chase, and the name of the game was to keep running. Eventually from a long way back I made it into the middle of a crowd and was safe. It was a wonderful concert from the best of the Beatles. I am sorry, but anyone who thinks it was that other chap needs their head examined.

By way of contrast, one of the most recent concerts I went to was Elton John at Mount Smart Stadium in 2020. I'd changed, and so had he, from the several other times I'd seen him. Here's the thing. Unlike at Paul McCartney, I was sitting, not standing; unlike at Paul McCartney, I took my family (save the littlest child); and unlike at Paul McCartney, I paid hundreds – like about $400 – per ticket, so that Elton got a cool $1600 or something out of my purse. Oh and unlike Sir Paul, neither Sir Elton nor his band was all that good. Yes, I appreciate he was unwell, but he didn't finish the concert and we didn't get any refund. London florists cost a lot of money, I understand.

In my thirties as a new MP, then as a minister with kids, there wasn't a lot of live music in my life. It was a period of artistic stasis for me. One side of my brain did all the working out while the other half slept. But when I hit forty, Natalie and I resolved we needed more soul and tunes in our lives. Now we get to quite a lot of live acts and, off the top of my head, I've greatly enjoyed a bunch of top performers: U2 (again), Simply Red, Roxy Music, John Mayer, the Foo Fighters, Sting, Paul Simon, Maroon 5, Adele and AC/DC. Soul, pop, hard rock. It's all been great.

That said, there is nothing quite like a little jazz bar, and I abhor the lack of them in New Zealand today. As a university student and then young lawyer, I would often frequent the now long gone London Bar on Wellesley Street for a pint or three and some good Auckland jazz. They were great times. I also still remember my international trips from the little jazz bars I have found on them, whether Tokyo, Bangkok or Oregon. A few roasted nuts, a Bloody Mary and some artists tapping away on drums, piano and maybe some brass is nirvana – or actually an oasis, like finding water and a palm tree for shade and refreshment after time in the hot desert sun.

Music has been a big thing for me, a bit like sport for others, since as long as I can remember. I have always had tunes and rhythms running through my head. And I've always been around it physically. Being in a holy rolling church helps. There are always musos and equipment around – a base, a piano and a drumkit to hack at.

At our church there were two big deals: Dad's fire-and-brimstone preaching, and the music. The music had to be good to draw people in to hear and meet Jesus. Dad got in a great music leader and assistant pastor, Dan Stradwick. Dan had been the lead guitarist for Ray Woolf back in the day and had music in him from head to toe, as did all his children, who were around my age and my best mates at the time. With them we started little jazz jam sessions slightly before I hit puberty – John Strad on bass, his dad on piano and me on the drums. I was terrible but persistent, and over time I improved a lot.

I started the drumming with some cassette tapes someone gave me with a few basic beats laid down. I would slot the tape into my brother Mark's Sony Walkman and through the headset hear the beats. I would then practise hour after hour on the church Pearl set until I had them down. *Dom ba, dom dom ba / dom ba, dom dom ba / Da dom ba, dom dom ba / Da dom ba, dom dom ba.*

I also began getting lessons. Over the years these were from a variety of drummers of varying quality. There was one old Def Leppard–style rocker I would cycle to in Henderson after school. It was a long bike ride but I was committed.

He was a bit grumpy, I suspect as a result of his sessions not just on the kit but on the Jack and colas as well, and yet he was a good drummer, taught me to read drum music, and tuned me up into a proficient rock musician. Another older man I went to lived at the back of Te Atatū Peninsula. He was originally from Switzerland and, while he could have passed for an accountant, he was a remarkable drummer who learned his craft at a traditional drumming academy back home when he was young. I never actually saw him work a kit, but I understand he was both a terrific jazz drummer and alternative percussionist. He taught, working just on the snare drum or a practice pad to save our ears. He was able to do drum rolls and the like so fast you couldn't even see his hands move. He would start slow then move to machine-gun pace before going so fast on the snare it sounded like a hum, so indiscernible were the individual beats. And he had complete control. He could do this at mouse volume or lion level, taking the hum from a gentle *zzzzzzzzzz* to a gigantic roar. This drumming was in what he and the drumming world call paradiddles: double, triple, et cetera. By the end I was pretty good and this added a proficiency and polish to my drumming that certainly wasn't there before.

Through this time I was playing drums at church services and then eventually in bands. I was part of a metal band entering the Smokefree Rock Quest, as well as a little jazzy group. I did community musicals in the orchestra pit and then at some point later in my teens I connected with friends of friends in a cover band where we played at a range of twenty-firsts and balls. I improved even more and over time, in addition to the other part-time jobs I had, I was making money.

In reality much of the money was probably reinvested back into my drumkit, a nice little Pearl set, along with thousands of dollars of cymbals, mainly Zildjian for those of you in the know. I had splash, crash and china cymbals, ride cymbals and more crashes. The kit and accompaniments were my pride and joy until I sold it all at the end of varsity to pay for my OE. If I had paid, I dunno, five or six grand for all the hardware new, I am not sure I broke two thousand on the resale. Only in recent times have I again gone back to drums and drumkits. On losing the leadership of the National Party I purchased my first electronic kit, which sits in my man cave out the back of my garage with a drum amp. While my speed and fluency is nothing like it used to be, I put on soulful tunes and feel alright as I play along.

I certainly don't want to claim I was Phil Collins, but I was good. Music has come naturally and with application has been important to me. Phil of course has nearly crippled himself through dedication to his beats. I can't claim that, but I did need an operation to remove a spur from the elbow I used to strike the snare drum as a young man. I am sure this impact was what did it for me and why I needed the orthopaedic surgeon's knife.

Alongside all of this crashing and splashing, I was also a closet aficionado of another genre: classical. Strange for a working-class boy out West I know, but two or three things led to this and to a lifelong love affair with the likes of Pyotr Ilyich Tchaikovsky and Gustav Mahler.

As a very young child in preschool, somehow I came across my mum's old classical records. They were nothing special – the one I remember was a sort of a top twenty classical hits album. I became mesmerised and in particular by one tune that these days I don't go much on but which appealed so greatly back then: 'William Tell Overture' by Rossini. I played it over and over and over. I played it so much so that the record became all scratched and would jump about wildly like a cricket in the rain. What's more, I didn't just listen. I was an active participant, standing on a stool with Mum's knitting needles in hand, gesticulating manically as I conducted that big imaginary orchestra, each member of which was entirely at my beck, my call, my whim. Violinists, flautists, the brass, the timpani. They all rose and fell, quietened down and reached a mighty climax to my knitting needles.

There was a touch of unbridled megalomania in all of this, let's be honest. But as I listen to this music again I can understand why. It's so grand, so regal and yet so militaristic and so primal. Even a small boy can rise to it. It made me believe I could lead an orchestra to crescendo or an army into battle. That overture still speaks to me of the visceral power of music to move children, grown men and little old ladies too. I instinctively got it as a four-year-old. Mum did too. It stirred and activated something in me that was strong, possibly even jingoistic. With that music going, I was ready to march to war.

Then as I was still conducting imaginary orchestras in my head, I went to the orchestra. My primary school, from memory, or it may have been Mum, took me into town to the Auckland Town Hall to see a man called Sir William Southgate conducting a symphony orchestra in a kid's programme. Well I never. What an eye-opener, a revelation as if from the heavens. From *Star Wars* to *The Muppets*, it was so incredible, so beautiful. I was hooked, and for a time I knew that when I was older, I would conduct orchestras. My practice with knitting needles moved into overdrive.

At high school Mr Bates was an English teacher who helped the debating team, which I captained. Silly students would call him 'master' instead of 'mister' because of the juvenile effect of combining 'master' with his surname. Anyway, he helped broaden my interest further. Mr Bates had a deep bassoon-like voice and sang with Auckland Opera. I would go with Mum to hear him in the choir. I went more than once to the Civic Theatre and remember *Carmen*. What a marvel. Beef-cake men with booming voices. Bosomed women with beautiful songs. Singing in some language I didn't understand but with an emotion, theatricality and musicality I did. Like another act of love, it's an internationally understood language.

Over time as a school, then university, student I became relatively regular at the opera, up in the Gods at St James and the Civic. It was a reprieve from reality into a new, higher plain. There was the likes of *La traviata*, *La bohème*, *Turandot* and more. Today I still have a love for classical music and opera, mainly the impressionists and romantics from the nineteenth and early twentieth centuries like Claude Debussy and Maurice Ravel. I still go to a concert every few months, though not more regularly because, frankly, they sadden me. It's not what actually occurs on stage – it's like all the world and heavens colliding in a good way – but it's the audiences that are depressing.

Each concert, while crying out for larger crowds of everyday New Zealanders, tragically seem to have the same old people each time: lecturers I recognise from university days and a few RNZ types I know of. What a tragedy. A bit like what happened to New Zealand First: what happens when they all die off? Will the party and the concerts also wither? We need to democratise this wonderful work for the classical music lovers of tomorrow. Our NZSO and ASO are such treasures and shouldn't be performing again and again to the same crowd. They deserve and need a wider viewing. I don't blame the orchestras. But I could possibly blame the government. After all, Jacinda's team went to cancel Concert FM until the outcry was too great. While Helen got it, I am not sure the new management do. Are Philistines at the gate more interested in youth stations than keeping the best of our culture alive?

Possibly I am being unfair. More likely the blame lies with middle New Zealand and a cultural complacency and malaise that rests over our nation like a low-hanging cloud. Land of the long, complacent cloud, it seems. All round the world, orchestral music is an acquired taste. I'm sure that many other countries, such as the US and Australia, have in their culture too an anti-elitist, anti-intellectual and anti-artistic bent that gets in the way of the masses going highbrow. I do wonder if it's even worse here, though.

In the main we are supremely ignorant of our history, and musical history and culture are to be included in that. What's worse, we don't seem concerned to learn. Interests within government seem keen to throw money at youth stations, while our orchestras are low priorities and low profile in comparison. I know that the NZSO and ASO have youth programmes and seek to inculcate the coming generations. I've resolved to take my kids; I know they'll love it.

Having been a little mean about my poor old dad at times, I should also credit him with rounding out my musical education with one other oeuvre: musical theatre. Dad, like a child in many ways, loved the action and energy of a musical and, hence, we went to quite a few. Anything by Andrew Lloyd Webber: *Cats, Joseph and the Amazing Technicolor Dreamcoat, Jesus Christ Superstar, Evita, The Phantom of the Opera.* Whenever an international troop came, Dad found the money and we went. *Fiddler on the Roof, Chicago* and *Les Misérables* also spring to mind. I recollect it was just him, Mum and me, not any other brothers or sisters, probably because I was too young to leave home and a bit spoilt as the youngest.

In time I got into school shows. The main one in my time at Rutherford College was *Oliver!*, in which I played the friendly undertaker, Mr Sowerberry. I did an awkward dance and song with my on-stage wife, real name Anika. The problem was that Anika was bigger than me, with me only coming up to her chest. It kind of worked, kind of didn't. Today as a local MP I still see a few shows, mainly amateur productions. Good harmless fun.

I also try and give our three kids a wide variety of experiences. We haven't yet, but we will go to the orchestra. The older two learn instruments, and all three – the two boys and our little girl – go to ballet class, which has its own special kind of musicality. In the car when we've been travelling around, all three kids have insisted on their music rather than our adult beats. The boys in particular acted like terrors if we didn't put on what they wanted, screaming and wailing until they got their way. So I have tried to ensure it's, yes, The Wiggles and *Sesame Street* and other garden variety nursery rhymes, but also some interesting and unusual stuff that's age appropriate. For example, we got Emlyn a CD called *Baby Jazz*. It's just what the title implies: soulful jazzy sounds in saxophone and ivory for minors. He adored it.

Speaking of The Wiggles, having helped get them into the country in 2021 when the promoter wrote to me as a local MP, I thought I had better go along to the show. The boys had been before but Jemima hadn't. So with Tauranga being fully booked, Natalie, Jemima and I went along to the Hamilton concert. Well, the kids loved it. While I don't exactly get it, they do and that's what matters. They are, I suppose, very catchy tunes – annoyingly so, as after Jemima has watched The Wiggles on Netflix, no one can get the songs out of their heads for hours afterwards. The other thing I would say is that, while I have never taken illicit drugs, I imagine that, as an adult, seeing a Wiggles show with a couple of psychoactive substances under one's belt might be the way to go. I wonder if that also applies to the performers on stage, such are their smiles and joy singing 'Hot Potato' for the 23,000th time. That said, when their cheap-seat tickets are $45 each for precisely one hour onstage, that would flick a smile on my dial too, illicit drugs or not.

From personal experience I can authoritatively say music and politics don't really cross over too much in the Venn diagram of life. Bill Clinton got the American public to love him by playing the sax on *Saturday Night Live*, and the US has a culture of big musicians coming out on one side of politics. We don't really have these musical political traditions. I can say from first-hand experience that while John Key has many talents, singing and musicality aren't among them. Bill English, don't know. Jacinda of course has been a DJ, but it's hard to really know if that means she has any musical ability or not. I acknowledge some DJs are hugely gifted, but some are just mixing other people's music. Surely anyone with some training, a vague sense of timing and a volume knob can do that.

My drumming has come in handy as a retail politician the odd time. In one video we used at National's 2018 conference, I laid the drums for the music. We hired some Auckland session studio and, in twenty minutes with a bassist, we were done. At the conference I walked on stage to the video – it went down a treat live on the TV that night, and as a video it was seen 450,000 times on Facebook alone. The power of music. Its main purpose was to show a different side to me. I wasn't just a hard-ass, tough-guy politician. And funnily enough, people on the street, whether I am in Invercargill or Auckland, still often ask me about my drumming. It's a side of me that people remember. I've also used it as a bit of a prop at the odd event. After a robust public meeting in Hastings at a church, somehow I ended up on the drums. Well of course it was the main story from the day. The drumming is still up on the *Herald*'s website, showing off my fairly rusty stick skills.

An ability to approximately sing in tune has also come in handy the odd time. At a Filipino function in Tauranga, I was pressured to join in the karaoke. I did a little Elvis – a safe choice, as crooning in a low key isn't too difficult. I should have appreciated that smartphones, particularly in a Filipino crowd geared up for selfies with politicians, would come out. It went viral and made it to TV. Once again, the power of music, social and mainstream media were all working for me.

When we think about music and our identity, having made the case for classical music as part of our cultural DNA, I wouldn't want it thought that I am somehow against what's happening in our country's modern scene: Lorde, Benee, Six60, L.A.B. Despite the fact that most of these artists probably despise National and me, I acknowledge it's a pretty dynamic and exciting scene, even if I am entirely underqualified to commentate on it. New Zealand's contemporary music world is varied and vibrant. To coin the hackneyed phrase, we do punch above our weight in this arena.

It would also be remiss not to mention our Indigenous sounds. Māori and Pasifika have contributed a huge amount to our music scene. From the Howard Morrisons to the Prince Tui Tekas and even the likes of Billy T James, Māori have changed the sound of mainstream music here. While it's probably more properly a PhD topic at a university, I'd say Polynesian rhythm and also that inimitable acoustic guitar style (*ginga chek, ja ginga chek*) have had a disproportionate influence on all New Zealand music, from Dave Dobbyn through Split Enz and more.

This in turn brings me to Pākehā music. What does quintessential Kiwi pop or rock sound like? A case could be made for the Finn brothers and their work with other great artists in Split Enz and then Crowded House. But I can't help but reflect that Crowded House, with at least a couple of Aussies, possibly feels more at home at the Sydney Opera House than at the Auckland Domain. They're perhaps Australasian. Then there is Dave Dobbyn, a sublime New Zealand musician. Sir Dave strikes me as, quite self-consciously, a Kiwi artist, with his collaborations with Herbs and more recently with the *haere mai*s wavering throughout his songs. I love the spiritual quality of his contemporary work. Whether it's songs like 'Forgiveness' or 'It Dawned on Me', a clear meditation on God and nature, his is gospel music today, Kiwiana style.

But for me, probably given time-of-life factors like where I have seen them play, I reckon The Exponents are New Zealand's band. Jordan Luck at the Powerhouse, or up at Paihia over summer, feels as quintessentially Aotearoa as it comes. The Exponents' *Something Beginning with C* album was a coming-of-age cassette for me, coinciding with my hormonal teenage years. Others born before or after me no doubt will have a different national band. Maybe those just a few years younger than me would say Supergroove. Maybe those in their twenties would say Lorde, and maybe teens today would say Benee. But this is my book and so I get to make the rules. The Exponents are New Zealand's band, okay?

13
NATURE

ONE YEAR IN THE MID-2000S, AROUND MAY, I TRAMPED LAKE Waikaremoana in the remote Te Urewera in the North Island. It was me, Natalie and a couple of pals of mine, Peter and Richard. Natalie was new to the world of tramping and to the outdoors.

We drove there in one of the guys' old Subaru. Past the last town, Murupara, you hit gravel on a road that I believe Tūhoe hope to seal one day. We gently ambled along. Slowly, imperceptibly, things shift from the New Zealand most of us know into another world. A wilder one, more country and western than European western. But with a touch of the bewitched, or Narnia or something. Misty and mystical. As we wound our way inward on the gravel road, at a point you'd see something. Then it was gone. What was it in the distance? Was it hiding? A pixie? A valkyrie? Were my eyes playing tricks on me?

Then she would slowly come into focus: a Māori child bareback on a horse. In a bit there would be another one, maybe without a shirt, then another with a bandana over his face. Children of the mist. Not wanting to be seen. Wanting to be seen. I don't know.

I had some familiarity with this area and its people, at least in an academic sense, and that was some sense more than anyone else in our Japanese stationwagon. As a lawyer I'd done a few Te Urewera cases, my firm handled the Crown cases in this geographic area, entering into Tūhoe lands. Early on, I'd done a heap of Māori sovereignty appeals, where someone might have been convicted of drink-driving and then appealed to the High Court on some variation of the line that Her Majesty Queen Elizabeth II had no jurisdiction here. It was a separate state, where Māori were sovereign and Te Queenie's laws didn't apply. In some of these cases the appellants went to admirable lengths to show this with their own royal seals, passports and other documentation. They never once succeeded.

Later, I also did a kidnapping case in Te Urewera where a Māori man had road-blocked and stopped people on the basis that he had appointed himself the warden, effectively sheriff, for the area. In yet another case from these parts, the charge was attempted murder. My vague recollection is that it was some intra-familial dispute where one side shot at the other. It was lucky no one was killed. But on this drive that Natalie, me, Peter and Richard were on, there were no judges and no police. In every possible sense, we were a long way from Mount Maunganui and Remuera from where all of us had come.

Eventually, we got to the isolated parking slot. It was late afternoon and we began tramping uphill to the Panekire Hut. We got there in the dark and slumped into our beds in the communal hut, tired out and ready to sleep. Other people's farts and snoring didn't keep us up. We were pooped. Overnight it snowed at the top of the mountain.

The next morning we set out with two or three days' tramping ahead of us. It began raining and never stopped for the rest of the tramp. Natalie began wondering why she had married me. There were moments of magic and camaraderie. The sights were spectacular with views of the lake, ethereal mosses and lichens, magical forests and mist. There were points where I expected a little elf to appear and sing for us, or perhaps a troop of Maori men, naked but for flax skirts, ready for war. But there were also ridiculously heavy packs on our shoulders. As a complete idiot, I had packed tins of food – beans, fruit salads and the like. None of this freeze-dried cuisine fit for glamping that I now see around. And we had wet socks and boots from rain, puddles, streams and mud. Our socks were sodden when we took them off, still wet when we put them on again. This was not a city girl from Britain's idea of romance. Natalie wanted to divorce me.

One night in a hut, Natalie woke with a weta on her the size of a rodent. She screamed and woke everyone. The next morning she wouldn't walk any further, but like the good stick she is, following much sweet talk and cajoling, we eventually moved again. It kept raining and it was cold.

By Sunday we still had a lot left to walk, but we needed to get out. Natalie had to be back at the Mount that evening to read the local radio's Monday morning bulletins. We marched hard. Eventually we were out, and the Subaru was still there for us. It had been horrible and wonderful. We all agreed, bar Natalie, that we would do it again but in summer.

On the drive home Peter was going a bit quicker than he had on the way inward. As we came downhill on the gravel, *clunk*. It didn't sound good. Then *shhhhhhhhh*. That sounded even worse. We were leaking petrol, as the Subaru's petrol tank had hit a rock and the petrol was slow pouring out. This was quite a predicament, but we kept on driving and I think I may have started praying. Thankfully there was a small miracle: the car kept going all the way into Murupara, and on Sunday afternoon we rolled slowly into the garage and someone called the local mechanic, who came, couldn't provide a permanent fix for the car, but could putty up the hole as a temporary solution to get us all home – to the Mount for Natalie and me, and then to Auckland for Richard and Peter.

While we let the mechanic do the puttying, I bought a pie from the garage and went on a little walk with Natalie. It wasn't raining, which was good news. A few doors down from the mechanic's was a motel. Motels as we all know are a great Kiwi tradition. Once for holiday makers and today for our homeless and gangs. But this motel this Sunday afternoon, while unspectacular in most ways, had something I have never seen before or since, and which made clear that perhaps those Māori sovereignty advocates were on to something. Some parts of our islands are very different and operate under different lore than others. At the front of the motel on the scruffy lawn was a massive tree stump, and into it was carved an intricate sculpture about a metre or so high. Someone had spent a lot of time on it: a wood-whittling of great skill showing a long, hard, veiny cock. Today I would have captured proof on my smartphone, but because it was a long while back you'll have to take my word for it. Were that in Tauranga, the council would have been called, the mayor would be outraged, and by hook or by crook that penis would be chainsawed down. In Murupara, the mighty erection stood loud and proud for I don't know how long.

From toddler age on, my family has walked in nature. Dad never came of course — not to anything and not into the bush with us. But Mum, or sometimes just the older children with me on their back or holding hands, would enjoy it. At least every summer we would walk into a waterhole deep in from Karangahake Gorge and also up a cliff from Waihi Beach to the neighbouring Orokawa Bay. Grandpa, Mum's dad, had been a Waihi dairy farmer and had retired to the beach. This was our free family holiday every year. We would spend endless hours at the beach, and I recall hours in the water unsupervised from a very young age. By the end of summer I was so dark that all you would see in the night were my teeth. We didn't seem to do sunblock back then either.

As long walks, both Karangahake and Orokawa were traditions, pilgrimages, to be done generally once a visit only. For Orokawa I remember walking up a steep track and then having to shuffle around the top on a clay cliff, a long drop to the rocks and sea below. It was petrifying. Then at the beach on the other side of the cliff we were forbidden to swim – too much of a nasty rip. We instead just, as with Karangahake, walked inland through the bush to a waterfall for a swim. One time I recall walking over a log at what seemed like ten metres above a stream (but probably wasn't). Where the log was rotten, I fell through into the stream, my head landing inches from rocks. I recall thinking I was lucky to be alive and running as fast as if I were being chased by a cheetah back to my older siblings.

In West Auckland my older brothers and sisters introduced me to the West Coast beaches, again while I was young. There were endless trips with them and their mates to

Piha, Bethells and sometimes Muriwai. Looking back on it, my siblings were great, letting little me tag along.

Piha – with the best surf, Lion Rock and black sand – was incredible. I remember once being pushed repeatedly onto the rocks and getting rescued by the lifeguards on the inflatable. Bethells was also a good surf, not that I was much good. I would bodyboard there and around the corner at O'Neill Bay. With mates from church youth group we would often go in to O'Neill of an afternoon and camp up in the trees in a clearing we had found. We'd make a fire, cook some pre-cooked sausages and talk some shit. We'd be woken early by real surfers running through our campsite. And eventually we'd also go for a surf.

Bethells Lake was a consistent favourite. Those dunes were like something in the movies, and so hot you'd burn your feet even with jandals on. As I grew older and smarter, we'd move around the side of the dunes by the estuary, which always reminded me a little of where baby Moses must have been hid by his mammy in ancient Egypt, among the reeds in a basket before Pharaoh's daughter picked him up. In the dunes you could find shrapnel from hand grenades. Evidently, the military practised pin-popping and throwing there a long time ago. We would find the biggest bits, sometimes a serious chunk of the casing or maybe the handle and pin. My brother Mark and I took them home. From the dunes we would run towards the lake, down, down, down the steep sand into the beautiful fresh water.

Muriwai wasn't my favourite, but it was still a great long beach. And the walk to the gannet colony with the bouncy bushes was O for Awesome. I also loved the Waitākere bush, knowing it, if not like the back of my hand, then certainly very well. What good days of endless summers on wild and wildly beautiful beaches. I can still see them in my dreams.

When Natalie came with me to New Zealand at age twenty-two, I was quick to take her out to Piha, Bethells and Muriwai. She recently reminded me of how, back when we met in Oxford, I would talk to her about these beaches, the wild West Coast and the bush. How I hankered for it while I was stuck inland in grey England. I'd promised I would take her. Though we were living in Tauranga, we didn't have kids and were footloose and fancy free. We would often drive up to Auckland, stay with my folks, and early in the morning head for Piha, Karekare, Bethells or Muriwai. In hindsight I think I needed to indoctrinate her, inculcate her in our nature, in my nature. It was part of me and if she loved me it would be part of her.

Prior to New Zealand, Natalie didn't have much experience of the wild outdoors and had effectively no experience of the coast or sea. When we met I had seen more of the UK than she had from living inland at Coventry, and so I took her on an English expedition up north to the moors in Yorkshire and out to coastal Scarborough and Whitby, where Captain Cook once ran as a boy. Well, I don't know if she had ever had so much fresh air in her life. Soon into it she was so ill that we had to stay inside as she feverishly got better. Then back in New Zealand I had her on the West Coast, at Waikaremoana in the mud and rain, and doing the Pinnacles in the Coromandel and the Tongariro Crossing, among others around the North Island.

The Tongariro Crossing is a walk like no other. In parts it's traditional Kiwi bush, but it is also alpine and volcanic. At times it's like you're on another planet, such are the azures and metallic oranges. On a fine clear day it's majestic; on a howler crawling at the top of Mount Tongariro ridge, it's a scary time. Natalie and I have now done it many times and have noticed the changes over the years. The first time, there may have been hundreds of people on it. The last time we went, pre Covid-19, it was a conveyer-belt of thousands. I say charge non-Kiwis for it. It's worth it in its pricelessness.

More recently I have begun taking my two oldest children, Emlyn and Harry, camping. I am not a natural camper – maybe I once was, but certainly I have lost the knack. I do enjoy it though, and with the boys and our family friends we did some huts out in rural Hawke's Bay recently. Our walk to the hut in the Kaweka Range was brilliant. Alongside the hut was a river with water so ball-breakingly cold that I doubt anyone could have kids for a while after a swim in it.

I don't know if it was a usual thing, but when we were there so were two stag parties. All good – the young men taught my boys some of their hunting and fishing skills. The *pièce de résistance* of the trip was about forty minutes from the hut, where we encountered some freshwater springs next to the river, proof humans can improve what God gave us to enjoy. The Department of Conservation had done a great job with some large tubs set into timber decking. Turn the handle and the boiling freshwater gave a bath fit for a king. From freezing river to boiling bath and back again.

Water certainly provides some of the best nature experiences in New Zealand. Like salt is to chips or a glass of red to a steak, water brings out the best in the world around us. Growing up with the beach and waves, that's primarily my thing. For Natalie, while a landlubber, as a child she did go to the Polish lakes to see her mother's family. All of us are our childhood, and deep dark lakes are her thing. She has thus taken us away from the beaches to the Rotorua lakes for breaks. In cold water, colder than the sea, she will jump in and before too long she's a speck to my eye, a long way into Tarawera, Tikitapu or Rotoiti. Natalie has taught me there is nothing quite so invigorating as a dip in a lake or river. The freshwater, the depth, is as refreshing as a beer on a hot day.

As long as we've had kids, we have always had a spa or pool at our homes. In the evenings we often get in and get to know the birds in the trees around us, from the scrawny old tūī to the small plump kingfisher. We are also blessed to sometimes see a family of shags and the odd kererū. There are a few fantails and a multitude of sparrows. More recently we've also lived under the rise of the rosella, those parrots I rather like for their colours but which I am told are a bit like the 501 gangsters, uninvited Aussies that create trouble and mayhem wherever they go. Certainly I have noticed in our garden that with the primacy of the rosella, sadly there have been fewer tūī. I suppose they feel a bit like the Mongrel Mob now that the Aussie Mongols and Comancheros have moved into town.

Once, around 6 am, when it was just Jemima up with me, we saw a ruru in one of our trees. I quickly snuck Jemima over to it and we gazed together in awe till the little wide-faced precious saw us and flew back higher into our trees, out of view. Jemima and I have this special shared memory and talk about it often: how she and I were the only two to see the owl. No one else knows for sure but us.

Late at night when the kids are hopefully asleep, Natalie and I will sometimes go in the pool at our home. The star-watching is pretty good. I seem to recall learning that stars are millions or trillions of miles away in other galaxies, and even if we were able to move in a spacecraft at the speed of light it would still take us years to get to them. This means what we are looking at isn't the stars as they are today, but stars from back BC, before Christ, only now reaching us by sight. How mind-blowing. Yes, the night sky reminds me how small we are both physically and in time. We are but a fleck of dust and a speck in time, or as *Days of Our Lives* would say, a grain of sand in the hourglass. Whether it's the kingfisher near us in the pool or the stars and planets a million miles away, these to me make clear there is a deity, a creator of some description. That kingfisher didn't come from some primordial soup or big bang with no purpose. There was an artist. Those stars don't light our night path with a romance and a wonder just because. There was an architect.

When it comes to our natural world, people the world over have an affinity to it and at some level derive their identity from it. There is beauty in every country certainly that I have ever seen. I do think, though, that it's an extra strong source of wonderment, pride and identity here in New Zealand. In the UK, for example, I know how beautiful its countryside is. But I also know how so many of its people are ensconced in the city that it becomes most of what they know of the world.

In Australia – no offence to my Aussie friends – the beaches are amazing, as are some of the rainforests and rivers and Uluru and so on. But in my humble opinion, it's not a patch on what we have outside our front door. Go out from a few coastal areas and, I am sorry, but Australia is one big desert. Forest fires, anyone? Animal pestilence? I've often thought that climate and landscape surely explain many of the cultural differences between us and the ockers (alongside the convict culture, I should add). A big, hot country makes life hotter and harder. Which in turn makes a people harder, bolder and brasher. Shit, they would have to be to survive the heat, the fires, the snakes, the crocs and deadly spiders. We by contrast live in a mild green paddock with hills and mountains, rivers and mud. This breeds a more complacent, kinder, softer folk because our climate and land make life milder, nicer, easier.

Our different natural environments also explain why Australia has been happy enough to dig up so much of its country for iron ore, gold, coal, opal and rare earths. They have mines so large they are seen from the moon – the Great Wall and Aussie mines are some of the more noticeable things from up in our atmosphere. Climate change concerns aside, historically why wouldn't you just dig it all up and grow rich? I mean, it was only desert before, not Mount Aspiring or glow worm caves or something. And it will return to desert afterwards.

Some of the bigger controversies in my political career occurred in my time as Energy and Resources Minister, as our government agenda saw us allow minerals and petroleum exploration both on and offshore. Firstly, it's worth noting that there was significant cultural and environmental consultation before we allowed anything to happen, and thus areas for exploration were always whittled down to smaller areas where, on balance, it was deemed acceptable. It certainly wasn't no free-for-all. We were pretty careful in reality.

The other big area for me as Energy Minister was a push into renewable energy. As I was always saying back then, we may not be a superpower in much, but in renewables we can lead the world. Our water, geothermal and wind energy is truly world-beating, as are our people who work in this area. This is why I have always felt that electric vehicles make such intuitive sense for our country. Why fill up with imported gas when you can plug in to domestic green energy? I digress.

On land, the issues around mining arose because, today, about a third of New Zealand is conservation estate. Not all of that land is pristine national park material – the stewardship land, for example, can be covered in wild gorse. As a minister I thought we could have our cake and eat it too: have our Tongariro Crossings as well as a bit more mining, with the jobs and value for our nation it would provide. It was surely a controversial agenda. It didn't matter whether the land in question was low-quality scrub, and I didn't help things with my occasional foot-in-mouth disease. One time, for example, I forgot the name of one of the forest parks I had allowed early phase exploration in (subject to further DoC processes and consents before any mining would be allowed). Well, the green lobby wouldn't let me live that one down. Russel Norman said I showed 'callous disregard' for our conservation estate.

Out at sea it was even worse. As Energy Minister I was responsible for the offshore oil and gas permits, and as we allowed such exploration in large tracts of our even larger Exclusive Economic Zone (one of the largest in the world), again the green NGOs were onto me, yelling that I was killing the Māui dolphin. This aggrieved me at the time, as we had put in place the strictest of rules and protocols for the businesses involved, including having environmentalists and iwi on board the vessels as they explored for any marine life. It was true that certain things were happening – and still are – out at sea that threaten our species and dolphins such as the Māui. But it was fisheries and certain practices on fishing boats that were doing the damage, not oil and gas, which was much more surgical in its methods.

Nevertheless, this didn't stop Greenpeace nor our primary schools campaigning against me. Teachers would have six-year-olds write in to me asking why I was killing all the marine mammals. This issue, along with Covid-19, saw me receive more death threats than any other. At oil and gas events, I needed security and police presences. Protestors often picketed, some even infiltrating the energy conferences to create merry hell once the events started. At one ritzy forum at SkyCity I recall a series of small mobile panic alarms being set off by protesters all over the indoor venue as I gave a big speech. They started coming for the stage, and so security and police swarmed. We waited for them to clear the protesters out before I finished my remarks to the large business audience.

I do look back on those days, if not with regret then at least with some sense that I could have played things better. I got where the protesters were coming from and the deep desire they had to protect our unique and special environment. It's not wrong to call our land and waterways our most precious taonga. I could have had empathy for the other side. I accepted then the passion of their cause and I could have shown more compromise. After all, I got then, and still believe now, that nature is at the core of New Zealanders' sense of wellbeing and identity. More so than most nations; more so than possibly any other.

We are all environmentalists and conservationists today, even if some are absolutist and some pragmatic. And we all want to leave our natural environment better than we found it for the next generation. I still believe there will always be a need to balance enjoying the outdoors with protecting and enhancing it, and that empathy and a spirit of compromise can go a heck of a long way.

14
SOCIAL MEDIA

SOCIAL MEDIA IS INCREDIBLY POTENT IN ITS IMPACT AND REACH. For better or worse it can make a world of difference to individuals, communities and nations. And to politicians, as I well know.

While I was leader, National polled opinion on the political parties every single week. In hindsight I wouldn't have done this – it was a throwback from the Key years – and I did argue against it at times because it can become a matter of obsessive focus as you watch the extent to which your party is up or down. As David Lange once said, you become 'poll-driven fruitcakes'. But the benefit of looking at polls every week is that you do work out what moves the dial with the public. I saw up close and personal how a good social media campaign on the right issue could move a party from zero to hero, and another from king to nothing very quickly.

I remember in 2019 when Julie Anne Genter, Green MP and at the time Associate Minister of Transport, went out to the public proposing a relatively complex scheme for incentivising greener vehicles with lower emissions, and disincentivising older, bigger vehicles through a taxation measure. I had no issue with green incentives; when I was Transport Minister I did a lot of work on electric vehicles that I am still proud of (paradoxically more than the current government, given their rhetoric). But I quickly saw the measures by Genter on utes and people-movers as a counterproductive tax on many everyday Kiwis, including poorer New Zealanders with bigger families. Farmers would take a hammering too, without the ability to buy an EV Hilux. I also recall at the time, for whatever reason, we were down on our luck polling-wise. A number in my team, MPs included, wanted to support the tax measures as they thought we wouldn't look green and modern if we didn't. But I spotted opportunity. I instructed the team to go all guns-blazing on social media against the car tax. We did graphics and videos and hammered them online. It sparked a huge response, mostly negative, from the mainstream media. But online, like nothing I'd seen before, we were getting hundreds of thousands of Kiwis watching – more, incidentally, than most media outlets generally get. What we were doing wasn't rocket science. We were literally lifting figures from Genter's document and showing the public the effect of her policy on the price of a given vehicle. The numbers were coming from her, or at least the Ministry of Transport under her. Well, the effect on our polling was rapid. We rose several percentage points. From then on in, we ran a number of other social media campaigns that I have no doubt were behind a consistent three to four per cent increase in the polls, keeping National's support consistently well into the forties.

Some in the team were squeamish. They wanted 'Kumbaya' with the government (and still do). The mainstream media generally didn't like what we were doing either. Some began writing columns about our social media and its recklessness. They were in full moral panic mode. Some media outright made stuff up, like that our social media team was now bigger than our comms and policy teams put together. This wasn't right. We'd built it up to two or three full-timers, all under twenty-five years of age, out of a total team of around thirty.

The other political parties also hated what we were doing; someone was putting around that we had media company Topham Guerin doing it for big money. What a joke. Those social media wunderkinds were off working for the Aussies and Boris Johnson – we couldn't afford them even if we had wanted them. In addition, the left weaponised the Advertising Standards Authority. Complaints began flooding in, seriously bogging it down. The left's approach frankly was vexatious. But nearly all complaints were rejected, given what we were doing was entirely factual. The one that wasn't rejected was where we had said the car tax could be $6000. Albeit technically correct, it was deemed too blanket a statement.

With the Facebook, Twitter and Instagram campaigns, we relied on organic growth, and so they had to be quirky or at least catchy in some way, shape or form. There were so many campaigns it's hard to remember them all, but I certainly recall them on gangs, tax, transport, general lack of delivery and KiwiBuild – our most effective one, as people loved to hate Phil Twyford and his pet project. It was a lot of fun. Social media became a big component in keeping National strong. And by hitting Labour's weaknesses, we put them on the defensive.

One jokey series regarded Labour MP Deborah Russell, showing how out of touch Labour was from everyday working people. Russell had given a speech in parliament in which she started going on about Ancient Greek concepts including *eudaimonia*. It was laughable, and we put it up online given the palpably farcical nature of it. Trevor Mallard, the Speaker, wasn't having it. We had edited the speech in a very minor way, and he ruled that we weren't allowed to do any more videos until rules were tightened. After a brief stand-off, we caved to him; we needed to keep moving forward, not be embroiled in a fruitless dispute. And, as I saw it, whether it was the positive effect on our polling, the media and commentariat pearl-clutching, the left's army of ASA complaints or the Speaker's position, we were certainly on to something. So much so that they all thought it had to be shut down.

Actually, some of what we did was heartwarming. During the early days of the Covid-19 lockdown, we opened up my personal Facebook inbox for messages. No other leader of a big party had or has ever done this. We were inundated with personal responses to the lockdown, and we helped thousands with their problems and queries around wage subsidy issues, getting groceries, clarifying rules around essential workers and travel, you name it. And some of our hard-hitting Covid social media really resonated. Our online petition to push the government into starting quarantine for those coming into the country saw over 50,000 signatures; it was one of our widest-reaching social media posts in 2020.

But I also saw social media go against me, and powerfully so. In fact, one Facebook post might be viewed as the beginning of the end for me as boss of National. It went up just a fortnight after the hugely successful quarantine one. We were in the middle of Covid-19 lockdown, and I was taking a fair amount of media flak already for driving to Wellington from Tauranga each week to chair the Epidemic Response Select Committee. We were all meant to be staying at home, but I felt strongly that I couldn't do my job as leader of the Opposition without commuting to parliament.

On 20 April 2020, when the government decided to extend the lockdown, I posted on Facebook saying:

The decision for New Zealand to stay locked down in Level 4 shows the Government hasn't done the groundwork required to have us ready.

The public has done a great job of self-isolating and social distancing. The entire country has made huge sacrifices to ensure the four week lockdown was effective.

Unfortunately the Government hasn't done enough and isn't ready by its own standards and rhetoric.

New Zealand is being held back because the Government has not used this time to ensure best practice of testing and tracing and the availability of PPE hasn't been at the standard it should have been.

The rate of testing for the first half of lockdown was low, work has only just begun on surveillance testing to confirm whether community transmission is occurring. Tracing is the biggest challenge and experts have identified major shortcomings in the methods being used by the Government.

This is a real shame as businesses will suffer further damage and that will lead to poor health outcomes as a result of the huge stress this will cause for a lot of people.

Rapid and easily accessible testing for workers with symptoms will be essential to give small businesses the confidence needed to get back to work.

I'm sure many Kiwis feel frustration that we still can't do many things Australians have done through the entire lockdown period, at great cost in terms of jobs and livelihoods, with similar health outcomes.

I now worry that the harm of staying in lockdown will be greater than if we were to come out. We will no doubt see a rise in mental health problems and stress related illnesses.

I also have real concerns about the delay in healthcare for some people, like cancer treatment, screening and thousands of operations across the country.

New Zealanders can be proud of the sacrifices they have made during this difficult time. The Government must now move as fast as it can to sort out the issues with tracing, testing and PPE so we can get our country moving again.

Everything I said was factual and, over time, has proven to be fairly moderate criticism. But the online response was like an erupting volcano. Every hour, thousands of responses came in. Within a period of hours there was 29,000 responses, many more negative than positive. The media commentary was also mostly hostile, and moved, as they often did, into speculation about my leadership and a challenge against me.

Clearly in trying to do my job and hold the government to account during an unprecedented time, I had underestimated the strength of feeling from 'the team of five million'. But I also have a suspicion, I accept without hard evidence, that the strength and swiftness of the response may have meant a concerted effort to undermine me. Like Glenda Hughes, a mate and Nat, said in a *Stuff* column a wee while after the fatal post:

> Manipulative misuse of the power of anonymity on Facebook was recently highlighted when a post, described by various political commentators as relatively innocuous, drew more than 29,000 rabid responses …
>
> Out of interest, I clicked on some of the more vicious attacks and discovered the profile picture of several commenters was not of an actual person, or where it was, the same photo could be found in a free online picture library. A percentage of the pages had no other posts and had been set up just that day. Also noteworthy was the sudden inexplicable major increase in followers who had just appeared out of the ether to link to Simon's page.[10]

The National leadership team looked briefly at whether we should ascertain whether bots or the like were making foul-play, but decided that we were better to shrug it off and keep moving forward. The cost of forensic work on things like this could quickly move into the tens or even hundreds of thousands of dollars. That wasn't a price worth paying.

I remember the moment when, after the Facebook post, on the long drive back to Tauranga from the Epidemic Response Select Committee, my chief of staff, Jamie, contacted me about a serious death threat to me and my family. In the end, off the back of that Facebook post, I received two independent death threats. I had learned long ago, when receiving death threats for my work as a Cabinet minister, that these weren't things to muck around with. Jamie rang them in to the police; both young men were prosecuted and then dealt with by the courts. I was grateful for this because, as a Cabinet minister, I had found police loath to prosecute. The words in these threats were pretty hard to misinterpret. One of these chaps was going to kill me and my family and feed us to the pigs. The other threat was in a similar vein.

Anyway, on the drive back to Tauranga I was very low. Here I was just trying to keep the Government honest and improve their Covid-19 response. New Zealand was all loved up, but that love certainly wasn't for me or my efforts. All I got was abuse and threats to kill my family. Why on earth was I in this politics business? Law had been much cleaner and more lucrative. I appreciated that threats and abuse were part of the deal with politics at the top, and I'd had a fair amount over time. But in 2020, needing police help for threats to me and my wife, I wondered why I was in such a thankless gig. Well, the gig as leader didn't last much longer. Shortly after that Facebook post, the circling wolves got the chance they'd long been waiting for and a spill was on.

As quick as that, I was no longer leader. The bedwetters won, many of whom in any event would find themselves out of parliament after the election, as our party vote nearly halved. I have no doubt that pushing hard issues online had helped National stay strong on the most important measure of success for a political party: its popularity. But it came at a cost for me personally. If I take, as one example, the social media I personally drove against criminal gangs, the media and the commentariat hated it. But I believed in it, and the numbers proved that ordinary Kiwis agreed. When we released our discussion document on law and order, to spruik it a bit I did a provocative tweet with gangs barking like dogs. I made clear we were coming for them. Well, the media frenzy that dominated news and views for well over a week was publicity that an opposition party couldn't buy. But the abuse and threats we received, and the required police presence every now and again, were a downside. As was the caucus squeamishness. Some took National's huge success for granted but, seeing the polling, I knew it was our relentless social media work holding us up.

In hindsight, one social media gripe I have from that period is that some MPs would talk to me about their 'personal brand', and how certain things that were good policy or good for the party just weren't on brand for them personally. So as leader, I would end up doing the team's dirty work. I had no choice. If I hadn't, our party vote would always fall, and a spill would be on from the two or three in caucus who were always limbering up for a challenge. My leadership was damned and doomed either way.

What I've just described is much of what's wrong in politics today. American conservative political analyst Yuval Levin wrote last year about how modern political dysfunction in the West stems from celebrity culture trumping institutions like political parties more than ever: 'The people who occupy our institutions increasingly understand those institutions not as molds that ought to shape their behavior and character but as a platform that allow them greater individual exposure and enable them to hone their personal brands.'[11] In other words, increasingly there are MPs for whom if it ain't on personal brand, they aren't doing it. In growing numbers MPs see themselves as bigger than their party, it being nothing more than a platform for them to shine on. To paraphrase one of my favourites, Benjamin Disraeli: Damn your brand! Stick to your party.

Anyway, after losing the leadership I didn't have the same problems. Party vote the most important metric to judge a leader by – no longer sat on my shoulders. Nor did managing over fifty MPs. And sadly, as we saw, if leaders today don't do their own pushing for votes, then others don't either and as the party numbers fall, almost inevitably, chaos and pandemonium ensues.

Left largely to my own devices, I started posting on social media about nice family stuff without thinking massively about it. But my oh my, the turnaround in numbers of likes and reach was phenomenal. In 2020, remarkably, of my top twenty Facebook posts, thirteen were *after* I was leader and the stuff I had done personally rather than via my staff. Most posts were non-political, just pictures of me with Natalie, on my birthday, with Dad on Father's Day, and cooking a Sunday roast. Nothing, however, prepared me for 'the yak'.

Natalie and the kids had pressured me to take a big holiday in advance of the election and, because I was no longer leader, I had no excuse not to take the time out. My sister Rebekah lives on a farm just out of Nelson in rural Richmond, with her vet husband, Roger. They'd invited us down for a real rural experience and we were keen.

In addition to being a good general vet, Rog is one of the best big animal vets around. Somehow, he had some yaks. Natalie and I went down to a paddock to look at them and she started videoing me with one of the baby ones, which was walking alongside me as I ambled my way across the field. I didn't think much of this, but we posted the video. Why the hell not? I no longer had any significant job title.

As with the Facebook post during lockdown, social media in New Zealand exploded. This time in a good way. The influential Zavy Scoreboard, which measures social media engagement, was showing my positive sentiment online exceeding even Jacinda Ardern's. Mainstream media loved it too – there were columns, radio stories and TV bits on me and the yak. I was billed as a social media genius and, politically, media were saying I was undergoing a remarkable rehabilitation from purgatory as a likeable, relatable human being! For a rightwing politician, that is something.

While politics is highly fickle, everyone loves a nice comeback story. And I did too. As *The Spinoff*'s Toby Manhire said, 'In the weeks that followed [the loss of leadership] something fascinating began to happen: like a man who had emerged from a suit of heavy armour, he seemed suddenly full of spring, unburdened. In a series of social media posts – most notably a stroll with a baby yak – Bridges was rejuvenated, relatable, at ease.'[12]

Today, having enjoyed the personal renaissance, I try to keep up a relatively active social media profile. When I feel strongly about something, I mix my motherhood and apple pie posts with some harder-hitting ones. It's both the privilege and responsibility of Members of Parliament to do so when their conscience tells them to. But different social media, it seems to me, has different purposes. Facebook hits a lot of people: mums, dads, grandparents and kids alike. Twitter isn't so much about real people who live in my communities or vote, but it is where media and commentators hang out. As an Opposition MP, I use Twitter as a quick and easy substitute for a press release, and to remind the urban wokesters I am still alive, and that there are people out there *not* in their bubble who think differently to them.

My favourite personal platform is Instagram, as it's hard to make pictures overly political and it's got a positivity and beauty that I enjoy. Whether it's looking at Yorkshire countryside or ancient curios found by metal detectors, Instagram can be uplifting if you control it right. Of course there are many other apps out there as well, from Snapchat to TikTok, but I am not sure I am hip enough to venture onto these just yet. I will leave them to Chlöe Swarbrick for now.

All of that said, let's not fall into the trap of thinking these platforms are not problematic. I've developed a thick skin and basically don't read comments on anything I post – social media is a one-way tool for me. But even so, every now and again the bile and nonsense do get to me. Even when you simply 'use' the mediums as platforms, they can still make you measure yourself by numbers of likes or what random strangers may be saying. What you pretend is only for work purposes can become personal and addictive.

For this reason, I try to make a habit of taking social media off my phone regularly and only accessing it intermittently, often from longsuffering Natalie's phone. She needs social media on her phone for work purposes, and so I am logged in on her phone as well. As much as I can help it, because it's never going to be perfect, I don't want my own self-worth and identity to be about my social media. I want to live life in the real world with real people I really care about.

I've also implemented other measures to keep myself safe and to limit time online. On my phone I have got rid of every app that Apple puts on automatically, and I don't add any others. In short, I've dumbed down my iPhone as much as I can. I've also turned off every push notification that I can. If I could, I would just have a 'dumb' phone for calls and texts only. But with work as an MP, I do need to be able to look at emails and reply in a timely way, adjust my calendar when out and about, read news when it comes out so I can respond wherever I am. And if I am to remain a high-profile MP, I do need to be ready to take a pic of a cute puppy dog for those Facebook likes.

The trick is to not be owned by all this. I don't want to be a slave to the smartphone and social media. I want to use both to make my work more effective and for enjoyment, but I don't want to, in turn, be used by them. I don't want social media sucking up time and renting a room in my head, as it periodically has done. My iPhone should be the tool, not me.

I see how social media gets to wider family and friends. Even on my favourite platform, Instagram, I know that the beauty and portrayals are enhanced by tricks and filters that can be employed to brighten and thin, and so on. As young (and not so young) people are bombarded with ever more unrealistic presentations of beauty, this has to affect their body image. Plus, all the lifestyle stuff must surely affect mental wellbeing. Everyone else has more and better stuff, and more and better experiences. It can seem like 'my life isn't as good as theirs.'

For these reasons, I want to keep my kids off smartphones and social media as long as possible. Different parents will have different views, but I am not in favour of pre-teens or even young teens being online. Frankly, if I can keep my kids off till sixteen then I am going to. If I need to, I will get them dumb phones so we can stay in contact, but they don't need all the other superfluous crap. Call me a dinosaur, and an unrealistic one at that, but my kids' self-worth and mental health are too important.

I'd rather every event isn't just a picture for Insta. My builder mate was over at Matakana Island just off Tauranga and the Mount recently. He said that in the space of a few minutes of landing there in his boat, some beautiful young women turned up. Did they want to enjoy the pristine surrounds they were in? Don't be silly. It was provocative pics in skimpy bikinis and then back onto the jet ski. He said that a couple of minutes later another group of young women turned up and did precisely the same thing. For one last time, call me old-fashioned, but I don't want this for my daughter, Jemima, as she grows up. I will keep her off social media until the last possible minute. Sixteen for the boys, maybe twenty-three for her.

Social media is with us to stay. Its power is impossible to deny: a tool for good, bad and everything in between. There is no putting the genie back in the bottle, and I wouldn't want to. But there is a case for regulation globally around tax, content, influence and much more. Listening to a podcast recently, the commentator made a glib comment to the effect that, in politics, the right likes big companies and monopolistic behaviour. That's certainly not my view. I believe in capitalism a bit like Churchill believed in democracy; it's the worst of all systems apart from all the alternatives. And I believe in competition. This requires good competition law that doesn't allow too much power in too few hands. Whether in government or business, power corrupts, and absolute power does so absolutely. A couple of centuries ago, kids were working in 'dark satanic mills', labouring to death in appalling conditions for big industry. But enlightened people – believe it or not, priests and politicians – made change and regulated the big industrial titans in the big industrial age. Today, in the post-industrial technological world, we must do likewise. We must put in place reforms to improve and enlighten social media big tech, the biggest businesses the world has ever seen.

15
WORLDVIEW

WHEN WE THINK ABOUT OUR IDENTITY AS A COUNTRY, WE shouldn't only think about how we perceive ourselves but also how we appear to others and how they see us. I suppose it's a bit like a guy on a Tinder date. He may think he's God's gift, but if his breath is bad and his stomach is hanging out of his buttoned shirt (don't look at mine, please), he won't make the best impression on his new acquaintance.

This matters more for New Zealand than it does most other states. We are the smallest, most isolated developed country in the world. We need others more than they need us, for trade and for security. America, for example, is so large that it can get away with being a bit insular in a trading sense. We can't. Likewise, come a conflict, we will never be able to do battle by ourselves. We need mates — basically, bigger mates — otherwise it's might is right and that isn't alright.

And if we play coy, it's not as if our bigger mates don't have other Tinder dates lined up. Australia has pushed its way into alliances; they have dating apps we don't even have the password for. The QUAD is a grouping of Australia, Japan, the United States and India. They seem to be doing more and more together as a foursome, hedging against that other newer superpower, China. Meanwhile, we watch from the sidelines. Now it's true that Australia is being squeezed by China at the current time. But Australia knows what it's doing, given my view that the world is becoming a whole lot more Hobbesian: frankly, downright dangerous, with political rivalries between nations beginning to override rationality. It's not that war is necessarily likely, but it's a whole lot more likely than it has felt for a long time – Asian Wolf Warriors vs the Dallas Cowboys. It's only for so long that New Zealand will be able to pretend this isn't happening. Australia is clear-sighted about its side and friends.

No one is suggesting any of this is easy. Of course it isn't. China is an ancient and sophisticated civilisation with a right to a prominent place in the world. It is our biggest trading partner by a margin these days. It's the golden panda. As for America, they, along with other traditional friends of ours (the Five Eyes partners), are now pushing back against China's human rights and economic abuses like never before. Can we afford the Five Eyes to be seen as four eyes and a blink? Can we afford to muck around our biggest trading partner? I say we do what's right over what is expedient, but I appreciate it isn't easy.

If you forget everything I have said in this little diatribe, do remember this. Military conflict isn't necessarily likely now or next year, but it's getting more and more likely. There have been skirmishes on the China–India border. In Taiwan, the tensions have ratcheted up and up. One misunderstanding and it could all be on. After all, were China to do a takeover of Taipei, it would be a massive backdown by the United States to sit idle. Could the US do nothing and still in its own view be the world's major superpower? If there were a conflict, would it stay non-nuclear? Here's hoping and praying so.

Let's for completeness not forget Russia under Vlad Putin. It's more malevolent than most countries, with the exception of North Korea. If you think I felt sorry for myself as Opposition leader, spare a thought for Alexei Navalny, Russia's poisoned Opposition politician. In the West, leading Opposition can be inconvenient. In Russia it's deadly, with an administration that seeks to rule in perpetuity and with minimal regard for international norms and standards.

Being small and remote, New Zealand is in a better position than most. But we would *need* a position. Abstaining is a weak, possibly untenable option. While I certainly don't hold myself out as an international affairs specialist, I've learned a bit over a few years in parliament and government. In the course of my career I've been to literally every continent, in some cases many times, meeting politicians and bureaucrats the whole world over. As a young buck, pre-Cabinet minister, I was lucky. Word got around the international diplomatic corp that I was a guy on the rise, one to watch. So every year, I got all-expenses paid study trips to the likes of Japan, Singapore and the US. This involved meet and greets with the political class, but also good times at tuna markets, feeding elephants and eating out.

One trip, my first, I will never forget. It was with Natalie to Ethiopia. I hadn't been an MP even for a year, and there was a system in our caucus whereby trips for parliament, as opposed to through government and for ministers, were divvied up. Someone needed to represent us in Geneva at this or that conference. Someone else needed to be in DC for the who's who forum. Well, as this was all happening, Ethiopia was also on the list. Two were needed from the National Party for the Inter-Parliamentary Union (IPU) meeting in Addis Ababa. The wise old heads knew this wasn't a trip they wanted. They preferred foie gras to sore tummy. But I thought to myself, I've never been to Africa. What a privilege. Nikki Kaye, also new, thought likewise, as did Stuart Nash from Labour. In those days you could split your business class ticket and take your partner, so Natalie and I, Nikki and Stu were on our way.

On arrival I remember getting in a bus to the Hilton Hotel in Addis. About five minutes in, Natalie was crying at seeing the raw poverty. It was hot, and there were flies and kids with massive bellies, clearly malnourished, running at the bus. We weren't in Tauranga anymore, Dr Ropata. It was brutal and very real. The hotel itself was like a badly run-down version of a 1970s New Zealand motel. At about US$500 a night, you might have expected better, but in fairness I think it costs a lot to get anything like normal for Westerners in these parts. Security was also required. It wasn't safe on the streets. Within days, all of us got sick. Diarrhoea was a given.

But wow. The coffee, the music, the people. The people were tall, slender and stunningly beautiful. To watch them dance was something to behold, like magic. And they were always running: a little out of the city, everyone was in training. Best long-distance runners in the world.

I wouldn't want you thinking it was all fun and games. In the daytime we went to the IPU meetings, the IPU being the biggest international state member organisation after the UN. People from all around the world were in their national garbs. It was quite something, mixing with chiefs from the Sudan, Colombians as well as Aussies. In the evenings we were on the cocktail circuit in huge secure enclaves – I particularly remember one at the British Embassy, a very impressive stone building, with cold champagne inside.

Singapore was also a trip to remember. After Bill English, at the time I had the privilege to be the only other Kiwi invited there as a Lee Kuan Yew Fellow, the thirty-fifth in fact. While Natalie didn't come on many other trips offshore, she came on this one, along with our first-born, Emlyn, as an infant. The Singapore trip was a luxury I hadn't really experienced before. We were met at the door of the plane, first off Singapore Airlines' first class, and then ushered to our hotel with a small cavalcade. As we entered the Shangri-La hotel, we were shown up to our room – or should I say *rooms*, as we had lounges and studies and bathrooms and more rooms. It was beautiful. I felt like Beyoncé or Putin or someone pretty spesh.

Every morning we would go down to the VVIP breakfast area and ask the chef for whatever we pleased. A little trout omelette, a side of smoked salmon. This would be followed by melon and berries, fresh smoothies and juices. All this as I read the international papers and felt just a little fabulous. Then we would be ushered around in our private car, yes, to a few meetings with the likes of the Foreign Minister, with whom I spent a day, the Environment Minister, and a few others as well. But there was also ample time to see the sights, to go where we wanted and spend the incredibly generous allowance we had been given. It was a wonderful trip that in truth did show off how impressive the Singaporean model and economy was. From swamps to front-ranking nation, all in a generation or two.

Towards the end of the trip, there was a special dinner at which I was guest of honour. The Chair of the Lee Kuan Yew

Exchange Fellowship was there with about twenty hangers-on, me and Natalie. I was expected to give a learnèd speech and then be presented with a gold-leaf plate engraved with my name and fellowship status. The slight problem was Natalie. As sometimes can happen in hot tropical climes, she wasn't taking it too well. Her biology is built for Warsaw or Wales, not forty-degree Singapore, even if we were inside in air-conditioned luxury. As I rose to give my address, I looked over and Natalie was looking pretty green. I didn't know what to do, but decided I had committed and needed to see the speech through. Part way through me talking, she excused herself to go to the bathroom. I cut things short and found that Natalie and a female assistant had left for our hotel rooms. She told me later that she was so feverish, so shaky, so unwell, that she crawled the hallway to our door while the assistant called a doctor.

Inside the room, Natalie managed to get up on the bed. The assistant, then in a panic, threw a blanket on her and spread-eagled her in a futile bid to stop the now-violent shaking. By this time, Natalie was rattling around like an alarm clock, afraid her teeth might shatter. I came up at around the same time the doctor arrived. He was a nice chap and his prognosis was that Natalie had simply got a rapid temperature, maybe from a virus or something. She also had diarrhoea, so who knows. One thing I do know, however, is that the doctor and the assistant had to hike up her dress and inject some good stuff into her butt. Not long after that indignity, Natalie was okay. She slept for a long time and woke up fine.

That said, with no medical insurance in Singapore the call-out doctor left a bill for 1500 of the folding ones. I reckon ordinarily the Singaporeans would have paid for it, but they'd quite accurately worked out that Natalie and I were stashing, not spending, their per diem. What they'd provided to cover fun stuff out and about was going in our pockets. Therefore we got left with the doctor's bill. In our defence we were a young couple with a Mount Maunganui mortgage back home. But in hindsight, we should have blown the cash while we had the chance and left the Singaporeans to pick up the tab for the butt-jab.

As a minister I did trips through Europe and North America to labour, economic, communications, energy and transport forums. And there was a lot of time in Asia, given it's our neighbourhood and where our money comes from. As much as I have hammed up the food and beverages and glamour of this, mostly as a minister it was bloody hard work. Early in the morning till late in the evening, pushing your agenda in meeting after meeting. You need to be alert and across your brief. What's more, a really good minister needs to know more than their officials and have a clear sense of what they and their government want to achieve, which will oftentimes be subtly different to what the officials want. I always had great political staff with me, whom I had handpicked, but I tended to go for workaholics. As such, not only did they work hard but they worked me real hard as well.

Then there were the sticky moments and the laughs. I remember MPs in the Japanese National Diet (Parliament) trying to feed me whale meat, and me laughing it off and refusing. I understood their game, given New Zealand's position on whaling. A cameraman was at the ready if I'd have plopped that blubber anywhere near my lips. I recall disputes about who would travel with who in which car seat and where certain people would sit in meetings. Hierarchies and placing are very important in certain countries. I remember warnings from certain government agencies about knocks on the hotel room doors in some Asian countries, whereby a beautiful woman would appear with a story and, when invited inside, the honey would be dripping and the trap set. I would lie in bed waiting all night for the knock, half in fear, half in hope. It never came.

Some of the better trips were with old mate and Trade and Climate Change Issues Minister Tim Groser when I was his associate minister. We visited Australia together a number of times to meet with ministers, align ourselves and share information. Tim was also a good tour guide of Canberra. Together we attended COPs, conferences of the parties for climate change. These were in a number of countries over the years, including the big one in Paris in 2016. While Tim could be grumpy, he was also incredibly intelligent, hilarious company, a great raconteur. In Paris, Tim had hopes of potentially being one of the inter-country negotiators, in which case I would be needed to carry New Zealand's interests while he was an international mediator and go-between. In any event this didn't happen, so we both had time on our hands – wandering the massive pavilion halls, getting lost among the literally tens of thousands of guests, and drinking red and eating steak and frites each night at some little French pub near where we were staying on the outskirts of the great city. We'd talk and talk, and plot world domination.

As Opposition leader, one does a bit of travel. I recall going over to see Scott Morrison, or ScoMo, not long after he became PM. Scott is a good guy: easygoing and easy to talk to. He also has a regard and empathy for New Zealand, having lived here for a time. By way of contrast, not all his colleagues are either easy to get along with *or* friends of the Land of the Long White Cloud. I recall one event in Asia where I had a bilateral with someone very senior in the Liberal Government. This politician arrived late for the meeting with me and feigned no idea who I was. By this time I was a senior minister in government, but this politician was asking me if I was outside of Cabinet or what. They then began talking over me, not that I really cared, but it was all very odd. At the end, the politician's guard slipped as they started mocking my degree from Oxford. This person had clearly read my CV in full and knew all about me but, as the bigger cousin, felt some sort of gratuitous desire to be a jerk. Aussies are a bit like that: either top types, like I've found in my meetings with Morrison, Turnbull and Howard; or real arseholes, like a few I won't name.

Also as Opposition Leader I did significant bilateral trips into India, China and the Philippines, all countries chosen because of their size, the potential for a relationship, and their large populations of expats back in New Zealand. For all three trips I took bespoke teams of MPs – generally myself and my Foreign Affairs spokesman, Gerry Brownlee, and then others such as Kanwaljit Bakshi, Jian Yang, Paulo Garcia and Mark Mitchell. I'd given Gerry the Foreign Affairs portfolio in order to buy his loyalty and happiness, and the trips were all part of that transaction. Fat lot of use in the end. Gerry was a fun companion, a good yarner. But for such a senior guy, Gerry liked hares and hounds and, in my view, he sought to run with both, voting against me in my upcoming leadership vote later in the year.

In any case, in each country we got remarkable access to senior politicians and government types. In the Philippines it seemed pretty clear that Rodrigo Duterte, the President, wanted to host us. While it might have been fun, I know how that would have played in the mainstream media back home given a few interesting views he has around drug dealers and the death penalty. I decided to dodge that media bullet.

I didn't dodge them in my trip to China though. I should have known. The reality was, some flak from that trip was near inevitable – a hangover from the Key years, where some believe we got too close to China. Of all the meetings I had, the highest up was with a serving member of the politburo, effectively China's Minister of Justice and Law and Order. It was in China's Great Hall of the People, which I can confirm is very great. The point of the meeting wasn't around his portfolios but about the bilateral China–New Zealand relationship. He could have been the Minister for the Great Wall, for all we cared – it was more about meeting with the leadership of the land. We didn't talk justice at all, bar me making some of the obligatory human rights points. Well, back home the talk was that we'd met with the secret police! How dare I meet with him. I felt this was all a bit much, really. Sure, as Chief Justice for all of China, he was in charge of activities New Zealanders wouldn't agree with, but he was also the person their system put up for me to speak to. In this big bad world, meeting with foreign leadership does not mean agreeing with their every utterance. What I found most interesting about the guy was his memories of growing up, sometimes without food in his belly. The older generation of Chinese politicians I met with often remembered this abject poverty and were therefore understandably very much caught up in the progress of China since then. The younger leaders, the new breed I met with, were much more interested in the here and now, and where things would go with the growing conflagration with the United States. China, I was told, would not kowtow.

For me, India was a highlight in those first three years of Opposition. Yes, it was an assault on the senses, but it was invigorating and exciting all the same. Every day it was high and low culture. We would discuss philosophy with the Foreign Minister and then be playing street cricket with kids. We'd eat New Zealand lamb at the best hotel and then street food, fried to buggery, on the roadside.

In addition to all the tripping around, there are the people you meet over there and back home here. There have been presidents and prime ministers from around the world. With some an easy rapport is quickly established and an hour flies by as if it were ten minutes. With others, just to fill the allotted twenty-five minutes is a marathon. And of course there has been royalty: from sultans to sheikhs, not to forget our royals. Regarding my discussions with Prince Charles, William, and Harry and Meghan, I had better be discreet. But I would say this: I found each of them much more impressive than might be thought. All, whether by training or their own inclination, knew a lot about New Zealand, and my meetings with them were not the chore that some of my diplomatic forays have been.

It's easy to be cynical about it all – the foreign affairs circuit here and the world over. I think it was Bill English who used to refer to their class as gin sluggers. We'd all chuckle and know what he was implying. But, generally speaking, I'd say we are well served by our career diplomats and politicians who globe-trot on our behalf. The very best of our people offshore develop deep relationships that can be called upon at times when we need them. They work those foreign relationships and systems hard in our nation's interest. That doesn't mean, though, that our political class has taken the right direction in their approach to running our foreign affairs.

If New Zealand were a Tinder date, we wouldn't be Ken or Barbie. We're more like some slightly overweight, middle-aged prospect who just hasn't taken enough care of themselves in the last decade. You see, as I have argued in other chapters, New Zealand is complacent. While the Aussies are getting squeezed by China, admittedly for being right but also for being brash Aussies, we sit back and watch the trade roll on and the cash register ring. Meanwhile, Five Eyes issues media statements without us, the QUAD doesn't have our phone number, and even China talked a little while back about plucking out our eyes. But hey, it's okay, we sold another kiwifruit.

I again acknowledge that it isn't easy. I don't think that right this minute we need to choose a side and stick with it. But one of our Tinder dates is at one bar and another is across the road at a different one. We are standing in the middle of the road, thinking it's all fine. Ultimately, we're dateless. Neither side is with us. Now critics will say, 'Simon, Simon, Simon, we have an independent foreign policy. It's a longstanding pillar in how we operate.' I am not advocating we lose that independence. The thing about Tinder is that people go on multiple dates: they're no longer exclusive these days, they're independent.

I just believe we need to be more proactive with our traditional friends, who are clearly on the side of moral right. We will still sell our kiwifruit and have a 'mutually beneficial' relationship with China, and we won't start yelling at anyone brashly. But we will be clear in our own minds about our values: that right is right, regardless of our interests and who has the might. History will remember.

16
RELIGION

WHEN MY FATHER WAS A YOUNG MAN IN THE 1950S, HE WAS AN accountant specialising in auditing. A more senior accountant took him along to a religious meeting where the first great American televangelist, Billy Graham, was on the big screen. That evening, Heath Auee Bridges found the Lord.

Heath's parents weren't religious, but as a child he had attended a local Hamilton Presbyterian Sunday school. The Billy Graham meeting changed his life dramatically. Dad kept working as an accountant but somehow, somewhere, he felt a call to become a preacher. He resisted and struggled internally over this, as he wanted the sort of success his mother Naku had wanted for him. He was good at auditing and in a good Hamilton firm. Then he heard God speak to him. A clear, crisp and audible voice told him, 'It will be alright.' Dad says matter-of-factly that he heard that voice and it was God. It had never happened before and never has done again since, he says. I believe him. What's more, I still believe in miracles.

Some will try and explain this away as either fable or a man's mind playing tricks on him. But I disagree. If a tūī can sing a song like she does and spiders weave webs the way they do, anything is possible. There is so much we don't understand in this world, even with all our scientific knowledge about our physical environment. Don't misunderstand me, I accept all of today's science and am incredibly grateful for it. Vaccines to combat Covid-19, solar panels and electric vehicles to ameliorate climate change and so on. I accept evolution, albeit I don't think it solves the ultimate question of whether someone pushed the button on the Big Bang. Anyway, I digress.

After being spoken to, Dad had faith it would all be alright. He left accountancy and went from Hamilton to St John's Theological College in Remuera, Auckland. Three years later, in his late twenties, he was the Reverend Heath Bridges and married to Ruth, who, like him, had also been saved. She'd grown up in an Anglican church, gone to an Anglican school, and as a young adult had a conversion experience at a church camp at Mount Maunganui. Then one Sunday she went with some friends to the Waihi Baptist Church, where Dad was the visiting student preacher. He saw her and that was it. They got married at that same Baptist church.

Religion has been a recurring theme in this book because so it has been in my life. I've always been haunted by that line in Shona Laing's song '(Glad I'm) Not a Kennedy', which talks about being tied up by a rosary. I'm not a Catholic. The good Lord knows there is enough of that club in the National Party already. But I understand the concept. Whether by choice or compulsion, I have never been able to shake my Christianity. It's more than cultural precepts to live by; I believe it and am forever tied to it. At times it's been all I've had and it has kept me going.

I hope none of that sounds overly negative – as if Christianity were an addiction one can't shake. That said, in some senses life would be easier for me in New Zealand today without true religion. Christians are the new pariahs in our society, criticised and laughed at, despite the fact that an overwhelming proportion of our social services work wouldn't happen in New Zealand without them and forgetting that, regardless of your religious views, Christianity has a leading role in our history and heritage. Of course, Christians haven't made it easy for ourselves. The Royal Commission of Inquiry into Abuse in Care by the state and church graphically shows the shameful behaviour that has happened, yes by a small minority, but nevertheless by the church in our country. And, in politics, any conservative religious party has to most New Zealanders practically shouted 'whackjob'. Remember Graham Capill? Colin Craig? Partly this is the reason I've never talked about religion proactively in public. It sounds weird. And more than that, I am not Jesus. I drink, swear and do a variety of ridiculously stupid things. Just as I don't see myself as a Māori politician, neither do I see myself as a Christian one. I am a struggling Christian who wrestles with his religion regularly. I'm also a politician, though not a Christian politician in the Capill mode.

In any event, I think there is a need for modesty about Christianity in politics. Not simply because it's unpopular, even embarrassing, and not simply because I am not a poster boy for love, patience, kindness and other milk of Christian behaviour. A Christian politician's every move is not inspired by God, which is fairly obvious if you watch me closely enough. But it's also that Christianity doesn't particularly inform my politics. The Labour Party was founded on a sort of Christian socialism and I could, if I really tried, find Bible verses that look fairly capitalist. 'Help the poor' versus 'If you don't work, you don't eat' – they are both in the Bible. I just doubt politics was Jesus's central project, and while I am saddened by the negative caricatures of Christians today, I accept we should be wary of politicians who puff out their chests with a Bible in hand.

Yet when I am asked in interviews about my religion, I always acknowledge my Christianity. In doing so, I chain myself willingly with the other outsiders who have done likewise. Jesus makes clear that if we acknowledge him in this world, he will acknowledge us before the Father at the pearly gates. If we don't, He won't. And He, in verses that scare me, wants hot or cold. Lukewarm and He will spit you from his mouth. I'm not equivocal about my Christianity. I am all in.

Note that I say *Christians* are the new pariahs. I am not mentioning other religions. For some reason, Kiwis today are more comfortable with religions that our culture has traditionally had little to do with than they are with the religion our country was founded on. Familiarity breeds contempt, perhaps. Or maybe Christianity's cultural closeness makes it more annoying and threatening somehow. Many in our nation have turned their backs on Christianity.

My wife and I laughed when we had lunch with a very wealthy woman a while back, incidentally with more plastic body-work than I have ever seen on anyone. She described herself as a non-practising Buddhist. Good for her, but we couldn't help thinking she was Buddhist simply for fashion and zeitgeist purposes. Her religion was a convenience for her, a pick 'n' mix from the shop she chose. I'd like to think my religious beliefs rest on something a little more substantial, even if inconvenient and awkward. I've chosen it because it's right.

Likewise, a corporate women's group that Natalie belongs to has had Spiritism nights of tarot readings. The women seem to be quite into it – I guess everyone is searching for spiritual enlightenment? But would they invite along a Christian speaker? Don't be so stupid! It's only the largest non-biological or racially linked grouping in the world that's provided people answers for millennia — so it must be a complete crock. We want shiny, fashionable and new, not tried and true.

You might think this controversial, but I take the view that we are all religious. Even if you are agnostic or atheist, aren't you taking a religious position? 'No religion' is logically a statement of religion.

In addition to the New Age zeitgeist that's fashionable at the moment in New Zealand and around the West (as I say supermarket, convenience religion), a couple of other things are also going on. New migrants are much more religious than old style Kiwis and are filling churches all over the land. This isn't just a few groupings you'd expect. Chinese migrants to New Zealand are often Christian, with the Christian Church in China being one of the fastest growing in the world. The irony of this is that Pākehā New Zealanders think they are in the growing group, of those losing formal religion. The reality is very different: outside of the old West, formal religion — and Christianity specifically — continues to grow.

Overall, though, officially, New Zealand has become a post-Christian secular society. Your average Governor-General would choke on her cucumber sandwiches were a prayer or Bible reading incorporated. Well, with one very significant exception. In recent years with the public renaissance of Māori culture, most public events will have a religious dimension in a Māori prayer or karakia. I love this for a couple of reasons. Firstly, it brings some life and culture to our otherwise arid secularism. Secondly, I believe our tangata whenua are spiritually set apart and important to our country. There is an exquisite irony in what's happened here. Our public servants and civic leaders, who'd spit on the ground during a Pākehā's Christian prayer, beam like Cheshire Cats when the same is done in te reo. I love this. God works in mysterious ways and he clearly has a sense of humour.

Tahupōtiki Wiremu Rātana, the founder of the influential religious and political Rātana movement, was sitting on his patio just three days before the end of World War One when the Holy Spirit in the form of a cloud rolled in. He was overwhelmed by its presence. It spoke to him, changing the course of his life profoundly. Some thought him mad, but as with my dad's encounter, I believe Rātana experienced a genuine visitation from the living God. Rātana went on to faith-heal and live as māngai, a mouthpiece for God. He straddled the spiritual and political, with a Bible in one hand and Te Tiriti o Waitangi in the other. Rātana also contains the irony of bringing God to our mainstream culture. For all the bigger parties, every political year is started at the Rātana celebrations. Politicians from Jacinda Ardern to James Shaw pay homage to this religious movement that shook Māoridom spiritually, at least for a time. You of course wouldn't catch these same politicians at a New Life Church, but given the cultural and historical precedent, Rātana is one time we do mix church with state.

Like my dad before me, I was saved at an evangelistic meeting. For me it happened in the hall of Epsom Girls' Grammar one Sunday night, age thirteen. I'd grown up attending my dad's church just across from our house, Te Atatū Baptist Church, twice every Sunday. But as he'd say: Just because you're in a garage, doesn't mean you're a car. Being in church wasn't enough. The preacher at EGGs was a guy called Barry Smith and frankly, looking back on it, much of what he said was mad. He believed we were in the end of end times, the last days of the world. Dudes would be forced to have barcodes (the mark of the beast) on their heads, and great persecution was coming from a one-world government. Barry literally scared the Jesus into me, because if all this bad stuff was coming then I needed to be on the right side of it. I walked down the aisle nervously and repeated the sinner's prayer like he told us to. There was no electricity or anything, but I was saved.

I don't believe it matters whether he was right or wrong on everything. He was right on the main thing. Since then I have been a 'born again', my sins and foibles acknowledged. I have had my ups and downs and moments, but I believe that if I died at any time, I would go to heaven. Yes, I believe in heaven and the less politically palatable hell. There isn't light without darkness; we all know and see darkness in the material world we live in. For there to be the same good and bad in the spiritual world makes sense, I reckon.

One of the things that's kept me on the journey has been that, despite what I've been up to, I have over time had a sense that God is a personal God, there with an individual concern and care for me. Certain touchstones from the past serve to remind me of this and bolster my faith. Earlier I mentioned getting a job at Kensington Swan despite having been rejected. I fell on the bones of my bum at that time, and I'd cried out to God as someone would on a desert island desperate for a passing ship. He answered. I could give more examples around things that have gone on in my family and my children's health, but one personal just to me and my story will suffice: becoming an MP.

I'd been a member of National since my teens and, in the mid-2000s, was the electorate chair of the Tauranga National Party, with a hand in getting Bob Clarkson elected as MP. Bob is a likeable rough diamond, a property developer with a big local persona for having built the city a speedway, among other things. With another in the party, I visited Bob at his home and talked him into standing for MP. The calculation was simple: only someone with Bob's story and profile could beat Winston Peters, the controversial sitting MP. The central problem became that, once elected in 2005, Bob was not for party or parliamentary politics. This was by his own candid admission. He was a self-made man, used to a world where he'd buy some dirt, draw a vision of a warehouse on a serviette, and then be out on his digger making it happen. He learned quickly that he hated the slow bureaucracy and hierarchy of politics.

In the period of Bob's first term of parliament, I was hitting my stride professionally. Natalie and I had come back to Tauranga from Oxford and, for the first time in my legal career, I was beginning to earn good money. Natalie was too. She had switched jobs from journalism in Tauranga to work as a writer and then editor of a couple of fashion and lifestyle magazines in Auckland. This meant both of us commuting on the weekend between our Parnell apartment and Mount home. It wasn't ideal. Eventually, in the middle of 2007, we decided we needed to be back together as a married couple full time. Given how well Natalie was doing in Auckland, it seemed reasonable that I look for work there. It didn't take me long, and in September I accepted a great role in a big Auckland firm. I told my friends at my Tauranga firm and was about to make the move back to New Zealand's big smoke.

Then just before Christmas, it was Bob 'the Builder' Clarkson's turn to visit me. He set out why politics wasn't for him, how he had done the job of getting rid of Winston and now he wanted out. He would stand down, and I was the guy to take his place. No ifs or buts. Of course, I was charmed by the offer. I had always in the back of my head had the desire to stand for parliament. But, as I told Bob, the timing was terrible. I'd just decided to move back to Auckland. I left my conversation with Bob by saying I would think about it and come back within a few days.

God, I was torn. And so I turned to God. As with other big life decisions, I prayed about it. Yes, it was the worst timing possible, but then wasn't it always. I would always regret it if I didn't have a go. I didn't want to be like all the people I've talked to over the years with their 'I could have made it in politics' stories. I knew that, if I left this, I probably wouldn't come back to it as each year I would earn more, Natalie and I would have children, and middle-class comfort would set in and stop me taking the risk. As Elvis said, it was now or never. There was no thunderbolt, but I felt sure in my heart and spirit that I should stay and contest for Tauranga. I'd rationalised it, but also I felt it was a God thing.

I got back in contact with Clarkson. I made clear this wasn't tiddlywinks because I was kissing off a big job and dollars in Auckland. He once again pledged to stand down if I would stay in Tauranga. This was our deal. I was staying. And I then set about putting the consequences of the fateful decision in motion: telling the Auckland firm I was no longer coming, begging for my job back in Tauranga while I waited for Bob's retirement announcement and a new National Party candidate selection. I'd bitten the bullet. There was no going back. This seemed to be God's plan for me.

Then, catastrophe struck. It was around February 2008 that Bob's pride got the better of him. He informed me rather sheepishly he'd changed his mind, despite our conversations. He would re-stand as MP in the 2008 election, as he was the only one who could beat Winston.

If you've ever been in a similar situation, you'll know how gut-wrenching this is. You've decided you're over something and it's time to move on, just as I had with Tauranga jury trial work. But then you're mercilessly dropped back in it, having to repeat again and again the same old things you're ready to leave behind. This is where Bob's U-turn had cast me: I was Bill Murray in *Groundhog Day*.

Nevertheless, against all odds, I continued to pray. After all, hadn't God been in this fateful decision? One day I opened the Bible at a random page and read an obscure Old Testament story from the Book of Kings that I had never read before. It was about a woman who, after years of barrenness, had given birth to a son miraculously as a gift from God only to then later have the son die. She prayed and the prophet Elisha brought her son back to life from death. God hadn't given her the son to see him die.

I saw this as a sign. In faith I believed against all odds for God to bring my baby, my political career, back to life again.

Surely God hadn't birthed it to let it die so quickly. I didn't have the dream and the assurance from Bob for nothing. I wasn't to walk away, but to hold my ground. March went by, then April and May. Nothing, save for a general election quickly approaching. And then it happened, my miracle. On 8 May, Bob made public that he wouldn't stand again. He'd done a full 360 and had gone back to what his heart told him. It was suddenly all back on.

Still, nothing was guaranteed. With politics there are always events and decisions you can't control. First, in regard to the democratic selection for a candidate by party members in Tauranga, I had the inside running as local chairperson, but would the born and bred homeboy Todd Muller also enter the race? He would have been real competition, as it was always thought that one day he would stand and do great things. We talked by phone and no, he wasn't going to. I was up against the popular deputy mayor (and later mayor) of the city, Greg Brownless, and a couple of other businessmen, older and more significant than myself at thirty-two.

I worked the campaign hard and did a good job. Natalie and I had a lot of cups of warm tea with delegates. Her help was invaluable as we listened to stories about folks' families, what they wanted for Tauranga and National, and I then dutifully repeated back to them what I thought they wanted to hear. On 23 June I was selected by overwhelming majority of local delegates.

Then though came the second hurdle: actually winning the seat. In hindsight, people always think it was easier than it was, but initially I was up against it. As many a dickhead reminded me, I was a complete unknown, a nobody, going up against one of the most famous Kiwi politicians ever. Lucky for me, I had excellent advice from the get-go. Other than in public debates I steered well clear of Winston, and even then I was respectful. My messaging to Tauranga was that of a fresh face who would be there for the long term of our young city, growing along with it. This was a story he couldn't tell. I passed him by. After a whirlwind campaign, on 8 November 2008 I became an MP in John Key's brand-new government. A miracle to and for me.

None of this means I hold any Messiah complex. There have been long periods of my life where I have sought answers through prayer but the phone to the Big Guy has seemed off the hook. Despite my stories, I don't believe in dial-a-God. It's simply that I believe God is there wanting a personal relationship with everyone. I am not special.

Today I go to a 'happy clappy' church on Otūmoetai Road in Tauranga, not far from where we live. I go nearly every Sunday. Many think such places are filled with weirdo fundamentalists who want to release demons from you. But my church is filled with hundreds of positive people who represent a near demographic mirror of the community around the church – mixed races, some rich, some struggling to get by, some pierced and tattooed, some not, all ages, all politics.

An elephant in the room around this subject is that some believe National is being taken over by 'fundamentalists'. This is nonsense for many a reason. First, there is no conspiracy. The handful of us in National didn't get together and form a plan while we were sacrificing an infant on an altar. We each had our own separate, individual journeys to parliament. And there are no more evangelical Christians in National or parliament than there has ever been. More Catholics, maybe! But not more fundies. I do have a theory why there are a few, though. Card-carrying Christians believe in public service and so are motivated to do things like stand for public office. I grew up in a church and in a family where you did stuff. Homeless people would come to our house and we would help them. We helped out at church and in the community through outreaches as second nature. Doing the same in a political party is also second nature and is part of Jesus's command to be salt and light in the world. Today in my church, and all those around it, I have zero doubts the congregation is much more heavily involved than the general population in community social services such as budgeting advice, foodbanks, homeless shelters and mental health assistance. Politics is an extension of this, not to ear-bash but to serve.

At parliament, those who identify as Christian don't meet in any formal or informal groupings that I'm aware of, other than at a weekly cross-party non-denominational prayer breakfast when parliament is happening. It's very light and there are no politics – just MPs from different parties coming together to share breakfast and a devotional. I've attended sporadically over the years, as my other commitments have allowed. It's been one nice way to get to know politicians on the other side of the aisle and see them in a different light, as I am sure they do me.

Christians aren't perfect – I am far from it. God knows what I would be like, even more flawed, if it weren't for my Christianity. But with my personal faith and relationship with God, I know I am on a journey. Over time I am strengthened, as are my relationships with others, while I run my personal race and seek to do and be better every day for myself and for those around me.

CONCLUSION

I WAS BORN TWO-AND-A-HALF MONTHS PREMATURE. I WEIGHED just three pounds, three ounces (or one and a half kilograms). The birth was a bit of an ordeal for my poor mother; I was coming early and the cord was under my neck so that I was pressing on it, cutting off oxygen. In the ambulance whizzing from Te Atatū into Auckland Women's Hospital, Mum had to be on all fours to keep the cord clear of me so I could breathe. She was thirty-eight years old and I was her sixth child, the first and only by caesarean.

As a result of my eagerness to get out, my prematurity and small size, I then spent several weeks isolated in an incubator, receiving oxygen and food by a tube and separated by space and some Perspex from the world and others around me. After a time nurses could make physical contact with me for functional reasons, but Mum wasn't allowed. I was only discharged to my new home when I had nearly doubled in size to six pounds.

This strange experience has had a couple of lasting effects, I believe. Firstly, I am the runt of the litter because of arriving early and small. My dad and three brothers are all well clear of six foot whereas I certainly am not. Don't misunderstand me – I am okay with this. The amateur psychologist in me thinks being smaller made me tougher and more of a fighter. I've needed that in law and politics. And anyway, historically, short men have ruled the world. While presidential systems tend to elect tall and therefore 'presidential' men, parliamentary settings favour shorties. Mongrels, scrappers with something to prove. Most of our Premiers have fit this mould.

The other effect is psychological. My first weeks in the world were alone. Not exactly like the Kiwi classic *Man Alone* but child alone, certainly. Next to no physical connection, certainly not from family. Just me, alone, and maybe just maybe getting used to that, even growing to like it in a way that was habit-forming. After all, today I am very comfortable being alone and, as an introvert, best enjoy being at home in my own space, looking out through glass doors as family scurry around and I am stationary. A little like looking out from the Perspex I'd have stared through as a newborn, at nurses going here and there. Prematurity and early isolation offer up an explanation from the very beginning for me for my outsider status.

CONCLUSION

But it's not all about me. While all politicians I know have a healthy dose of narcissism, I hope that as I have worked through my ambivalence and struggles with race, nationality, class, masculinity and more, it's resonated with you and your story. More than that, I hope my reflections have made you think more critically about our country. We are all shaped by New Zealand; and our country is, like me, an outsider. It's not fashionable to quote Rudyard Kipling these days – too colonial – but didn't he have it right about at least one thing: our biggest city and our nation? 'Last, loneliest, loveliest, exquisite, apart.' If that's not an introverted outsider then nothing is.

We are a sparsely populated group of islands a long way from anywhere, and this has made us self-reliant and independent. Sometimes we are outward-looking, but we are also capable of being insular and, with that, ever so slightly complacent. In that regard our nation's character and mine don't always fit perfectly hand in glove. For while in my difference I have struggled at times, I've also strived to be included and have laboured for more for myself, my communities, city and country. I don't know precisely what the future holds for me, personally. Some days I would like to go the way our country has, with its Lifestyle Nation approach on which I have written. Natalie, the kids and I could sell up, move to the Coromandel, get a paddock with some yaks, a room with a view, and watch the waves roll in.

A couple of boardroom gigs would come along easily enough, allowing pocket money for food and wine, and I'd slowly, surely watch the sun come down.

But I would then hear my Protestant work ethic whispering to a bellow. There is too much to do in this country that I care about, too much that's still to be done. Whether in politics or public life more broadly, I have more to contribute. It matters too much.

Mine, yours and New Zealand's best days – glory days – can be ahead of us. I won't and can't throw in the towel. And neither can you. Each morning that I wake up, I will smell the flowers, slurp a teaspoon of concrete and get into it. New Zealand needs people like us: doers and joiners, active in our communities and our cities, forging our national identity.

NOTES

1. Elizabeth Gordon, 'Simon Bridges Has the Accent of New Zealand's Future. Get Used to It', *The Spinoff* (online), 25 February 2018.
2. Antonio Gramsci (1929), quoted in ED Hirsch Jr, *Why Knowledge Matters: Rescuing Our Children from Failed Educational Theories,* Harvard Education Press, 2016, p 70.
3. Ibid, epigraph.
4. Elizabeth Rata, 'New Zealand's Knowledge Blind Spot', *Newsroom* (online), 19 February 2019.
5. Ibid.
6. Briar Lipson, *New Zealand's Education Delusion: How Bad Ideas Ruined a Once World-Leading School System,* The New Zealand Initiative, 2020, p 9.
7. ED Hirsch Jr, *Why Knowledge Matters: Rescuing Our Children from Failed Educational Theories,* Harvard Education Press, 2016, p 20.

8   Susan Cain, *Quiet: The Power of Introverts in a World That Can't Stop Talking*, Penguin, 2012, p 4.
9   Simon Bridges, Maiden Statement, New Zealand Parliamentary Debate 651:732, Hansard.
10 Glenda Hughes, 'Facing Up to Facebook: Moving Past the Pettiness and Pile-ons, *Stuff* (online), 5 July 2020.
11 Yuval Levin, *A Time to Build: From Family and Community to Congress and the Campus, How Recommitting to Our Institutions Can Revive the American Dream*, Basic Books, 2020, p 6.
12 Toby Manhire, 'The Two-Step Plan to Becoming as Happy as Simon Bridges', *The Spinoff* (online), 9 July 2020.